277.3
H44
a

Hertzberg, Arthur.
        The outbursts that
await us.

| DATE | ISSUED TO |
|------|-----------|
| AP 74 | |

277.3 Hertzberg, Arthur.
H44        The outbursts that await us.
a

# THE OUTBURSTS THAT AWAIT US

**Arthur Hertzberg**

**Martin E. Marty**

**Joseph N. Moody**

THE MACMILLAN COMPANY, NEW YORK

COLLIER-MACMILLAN LIMITED, LONDON

# THE OUTBURSTS
## THAT
## AWAIT US

*Three Essays on Religion and Culture
in the United States*

## "TEMPLE ISRAEL"

First Printing

Printed in the United States of America

THE MACMILLAN COMPANY, NEW YORK

COLLIER-MACMILLAN CANADA, LTD., TORONTO, ONTARIO

Divisions of The Crowell-Collier Publishing Company

DESIGNED BY ANDREW P. ZUTIS

Library of Congress Catalogue Card Number: 63-15684

# CONTENTS

# INTRODUCTION

The most recent round in the continuing American discussion on church and state began in June, 1962, with the decision of the Supreme Court of the United States forbidding the use of the Regents' prayer in the state of New York. At once major groups within the three religious communities in America were embroiled in controversy and slogans were being hurled. As the debate progressed it became apparent that the real issues were not to be found in the conclusions that these groups were reaching, but in the premises, most of them hidden, from which they had set out.

With this in mind, the three co-authors of this book met in New York last October to discuss the possibility of adding something to mutual understanding of the interior histories that lie behind the differing responses on the part of Catholic, Protestant, and Jew in America to areas in which religion and culture in general interact.

These three essays are the result, and in them we have not attempted to provide a program, or to offer the reader our best set of slogans, but we have tried to explain why each of us thinks as he does in the light of all that has fashioned us. We hope that the result of our conducting these explorations in public will be that the reader will make a point of listening to the two writers who are not of his own tradition, and that we will thus be able to add something to public enlightenment on one crucial issue confronting American society.

THE OUTBURSTS THAT AWAIT US

# CHAPTER ONE

# THE PROTESTANT REINTERPRETATION OF AMERICAN LIFE

**by Martin E. Marty**

Four Americans lived, with their families, next door to each other. Inhabitants of one of the newer suburbs, each belonged to the executive class. Each earned about $9,000 a year and lived in a $23,000-home. Each had a college education. The parents or grandparents of each had come to the United States from Europe, had made their homes in the same metropolitan area. The four families had moved to the suburb with no particular high-minded mission in mind. In the nature of the United States economy, it was easier to buy a new home in the suburb than a used one in the city. All four families had children, and the suburban space symbolized freedom, opportunity, good educational opportunities.

The four citizens, with their families, were good neighbors. Their children played together. The men greeted each other over the sound of the power mower and occasionally swapped chitchat about professional football, their jobs, and other men's wives. The wives were on reasonably good terms with each other. While they had other dearer friends than their neighbors, they would from time to time have a cup of coffee together and talk. Both political parties were represented in the four adjacent homes, but these political relations were somewhat loosely held and all the adults could be described as political moderates. When the United Fund came to the door, each made a contribution; all were expected to attend Little League games.

Family A was Protestant; Family B was Catholic;[1] Family C was Jewish; Family D had no church affiliation. Family A represented perhaps 45 percent of the people in the community's religious makeup. Family B also found spiritual company in about 45 percent of the people. Perhaps 7 or 8 percent of the citizens were Jewish and a small percentage claimed no relation to any organized religious group. None of the families was intensely religious. Parents A, B, and C were concerned to give their children a religious education. Children A went to Sunday school, children B to a parochial school, and children C took part in the synagogue's program for children. Children D were not discriminated against because they were receiving no religious training. The parents seldom discussed in detail the religious beliefs which divided them, and were apparently apathetic in their own spiritual observances.

No visitor to their suburban community would have suspected that anything but great goodwill served as a bond among these families and their other neighbors. The men were gentlemanly; the women, ladylike, and children must be children. The families showed a mild interest in each other's belief patterns. If any of them experienced a hardship in expressing them, others would sympathize and try to help. Thus, if the synagogue experienced a fire, Family C would no doubt be invited to use the facilities of the Protestant Church of

1. In this discussion Roman Catholics will be known by their sociological designation, "Catholic."

Family A. Each family wanted to instil in the children a respect for other people's opinions. Everybody wanted to go through life with the least amount of unneighborliness possible.

Then *it* happened. *It* could be any of a number of circumstances. Any of them will serve as a parable of disruption. A daughter of the Protestant family became engaged to a Catholic boy and announced to her parents that, the laws for mixed marriage being what they are, she felt she should become Catholic. Centuries of latent distrust of Catholicism welled up and were reflected over against Family B. Or, it was time for a school bond issue election and rumor spread throughout the community that the priest had spoken out from the pulpit urging Catholics to vote against it as he was experiencing difficulty paying for his parochial school. Family B then came to symbolize disaffilation from the community's highest goals. It was Christmastime and Family C, joining with other Jews, protested the presence of a Nativity crèche on the lawn of the Village Hall; Families A and B reacted vigorously. Family D joined in by attacking the prayers and Bible readings which from time to time made their way into the community's public schools. The religious families reacted vigorously at such "atheism."

After *it*—namely, after the event which caused religious disruption—had occurred, no one moved away. As time passed some of the tenseness and violence began to disappear. Cooler heads came to prevail. It was found that minister, priest, and rabbi, upon meeting, came to some understandings which they could mediate to the majority of the community. Children played together again and men still shouted "Hello" on their way in from work; the women no longer coffeed, but they had grown weary of the custom anyhow. Each family smiled at the other; each kept up appearances, but nothing was ever the same.

What went wrong?

What went wrong to occasion such a visceral reaction concerning a religious issue among people who were religiously apathetic, educationally well informed and, by temperament, moderates? The issue would not be too important if only a few homes in a prosperous suburb were touched by such an issue. But Families A, B, C, D only make up a parable of a kind of interreligious tension which, if it is not growing today, is at least more exposed to public view. What is more, the tenseness takes on a surprising character. In the American Dream it had been assumed that "the more we get together the happier we'll be." That is, men and women of good will felt that the breaking down of old barriers between citizens imprisoned behind high symbolic community walls would bring in an age of understanding and brotherhood. That did not happen.

The four families in our parabolic community had many coreligionists. Family A had—if one's definition is sufficiently imprecise—the company of about 80,000,000 Americans. If there were that many Protestants, there were half that many Catholics, 40,000,000 in broad terms, to keep Family B company. While there may be only 5,000,000 Jews, they exerted influence beyond their number because almost all lived in the great metropolitan areas where the interreligious parables are lived out. Many people would count 60,000,000 citizens— men, women, and children—in the company of Family D. Within each family, of course, a wide spectrum of religious attitudes and intensities prevailed. But there were certain predictable aspects in their civic life, predetermined by even the more loose religious affiliations. The question asked of one suburb therefore is being asked the whole nation in the decade of the 1960's.

What went wrong?

Why were good will, generosity, and brotherhood not enough? Why were religious reactions, when tested, not so much cerebral as they were visceral on the national scale?

What went wrong at the turn of the decade, in the fall of 1960, which led non-Catholic men of good will to be por-

4

trayed as men of ill will? A symbol for the circumstance is
Dr. Norman Vincent Peale, spiritual leader also to many
Americans who were not Protestant. During the 1950's Dr.
Peale had become one of the two or three best known religious spokesmen in the nation. His pulpit, his books, his
columns in newspapers and magazines led him to have a vast
following. Proclaiming what he claimed to be orthodox individualist Protestant Christianity but in a version with all the
offensive and scandalous edges smoothed off, he had an im-
peccable reputation in intergroup relations. His gospel of
Positive Thinking precommitted him to see the possibilities
for the best in the neighbor with whom he disagreed.

Despite his reputation, something went wrong. While the
public will never know exactly what did and what part Dr.
Peale played in the incident, he did become a leader and a
public relationist for a meeting held in Washington, D.C.,
for the purpose of discouraging support of a Roman Catholic
for the nation's highest office. No legal barriers existed to
separate Senator Kennedy from what would be his right if a
majority in the Electoral College chose him. But a traditional
barrier did, and the men at Dr. Peale's meeting in Washington
did not want to see the tradition changed. While most of the
meeting's participants were politically conservative, their Protestant postures varied from extremely fundamentalist to extremely liberal or even "modernist." Could a Catholic
American exercise personal freedom as a Chief Executive?
Would he have visible ties to the Vatican and invisible ties
to religious commitments that would limit him?

When Dr. Peale stepped from the closed doors of the
Washington meeting and began to speak to reporters, his
reputation as an ambassador of good will began to take a
partly undeserved but permanent turn for the worse. Catholics, Jews, and other Americans did not share this widespread
Protestant interpretation of American life.

What went wrong? What went wrong when, in the latter
years of the 1950's more and more of the relatives of families

C and D began to grow restive over religious observances in public schools. For a century the nation's public schools had tended to take on aspects of the religious character of their local communities. Since more Catholics were either cooperative in generalized religious ventures or were in parochial schools, these religious ceremonies took on the color of a bland Protestantism. As America grew more sophisticated and urban, attempts were made to formalize these ceremonies in patterns acceptable to the larger community. Thus in New York the State Board of Regents prefabricated an apparently inoffensive 22-word prayer which could be used to begin the day in public schools. To Christian America the prayer looked harmless enough and it might even do some good to instil reverence and morality. But non-Christian America was still not content.

Eventually, as everyone now knows, one of the complaints against this type of activity reached the U.S. Supreme Court in the *Engle* vs. *Vitale* case. In June of 1962 the Supreme Court ruled that the Regents' Prayer was not legally consistent with the First Amendment to the Constitution. While some Catholics and very many Protestants were later revealed to be in support of the Supreme Court in this decision, what may have represented Catholic-Protestant majorities of popular sentiment vigorously reacted. It was widely rumored that "secularists and secularist Jews" were the agents pressing for the de-Christianizing or de-sacralizing of American public life and were a menace to the nation's religious future. Something had gone wrong; somewhere along the way the religious interpretation of national life was in need of revision. In countless communities a strong emotionalism suggested that Americans' religious viscera prevailed over the good will which the national mind was supposed to be generating.

What went wrong?

After the Supreme Court decision, the editor of the Jesuit weekly *America*, a man of great and good will wrote an editorial. In it he gave concrete and clear form to widespread diffuse discontents in the Christian community. He observed that the step-up in court tests, the new assertiveness of "secular" elements in the Jewish community, and a too-vigorous pursuit of "rights" were beginning to irritate the nation's Christian majority. He even warned that an increase in the Jewish attitude could lead to a new wave of anti-Semitism. This led to an instant response from the majority of America's Jews. Not that *America*'s editor was anti-Semite. No one made that accusation. But the Jewish memory suggests that an increase of talk about anti-Semitism can lead to its renewal. Again, reservoirs of good will were dissipated and something went wrong.

"What went wrong?"—this question as a symbol of a time of change, of frustrated expectation, is best exemplified in the legal uncertainty shown the American form of resolving church-state relations:

> One hundred and fifty-eight years of constitutional history passed before the United States Supreme Court first confronted the establishment clause of the First Amendment (*Everson v. Board of Education*, 330 US 1). . . . Last year, however, from the spring of 1961 to the summer closing of the Court this year (1962), no less than seven cases involving the establishment clause were decided, and at least three more await the Court's return in the fall. In addition, church and state cases in the states numbered twoscore or more.[2]

Four suburban families living out a parable of good will which fails when tested; four general religious clusters competing on the national level and finding each other failing; scores of court cases testing America's past interpretation of religious life inside the civil body—each of these illustrates the necessity for reinterpreting the national mission and *psyche* on the part of the religious groups. The "Peale" in-

2. George R. LaNoue in "A Review of Church-State Legal Developments 1961-62" in *Background Reports,* an occasional paper of the National Conference of Christians and Jews.

stance implies a Protestant interpretation of America; the *America* instance suggests a religious interpretation; the Supreme Court calls forth a secular interpretation. Which will best serve?

# I

The assumption behind my introductory remarks could be summarized by the phrase, "Good will is not enough." Good will exists among American neighbors and on a lesser scale between the large units of American religious life. In some senses it exists automatically, as a result of other processes in national life: an abundance of natural resources keeps us from having to be at each other's throats to survive; reasonably efficient police forces prevent anarchic outbursts; our educational system inculcates good will. Many more reasons could be cited. But in other senses good will must be cultivated in intergroup relations. Before we discuss those emphases which inform national life in a period when "good will alone" has failed to pass the test, it is important to see how far the brotherhood movement did carry us.

It is precarious to assert that brotherhoodism is an insufficient basis for life in a pluralist society. The impression can be given that if good will is not enough it is not necessary at all. There are dangers in certain tendencies of reaction against the brotherhood movement to create that impression. In historical phases, when a time for change has come there is the possibility that change be radical, that it repudiate the immediate past. So a cult of hard-boiled pragmatists in the interfaith field may find it necessary to define itself over against the men of good will who carried the first phase of relations in an exposed society "up from the jungle."

Neighborliness, brotherhood, good will—these are not minor virtues and they may themselves incarnate many of the highest features of the highest religion. Without these virtues the newer emphases in a time of church-state or church-church or church-synagogue relations may become only a movement in which powerful forces interplay on practical, tactical grounds. When men wish to engage in conversation about differences it matters tremendously whether or not they are friends; whether or not their past experience has committed them to care for each other; whether or not they are ready to accept each other at face value and for their words' worth. No one who has attended any of the modern meetings where conflict is aired can fail to recognize how important mood and climate coupled with personal concern matter among men who differ in their ultimate commitment.

Here it is only necessary to assert that good will is not enough by itself; it is not enough unless it is coupled with some historical understanding, some theoretical application, and some technical awareness. Good will may be a major virtue but, as our opening parables suggest, if uninformed it cannot pass certain tests. Other forces in personal life and society are stronger. When "my" tax money is to go for the support of another religion or when "my" personal freedom may be limited by the claims of another religious group, the situation can evoke from my depths, my viscera, a whole pattern of ugly and contradictory emotions. This ugliness is particularly apparent when it appears in the collective representations, the larger associations and power movements in life—such as church, synagogue, or religious council or club.

To perceive the acknowledged change from emphasis on brotherhood to emphasis on practical considerations and theoretical bases it is profitable to examine the history of the national organization most competently involved in both periods. The National Council of Christians and Jews was organized decades ago when the older ghetto walls and parish barriers were beginning to break down and some primeval patterns of ugliness and prejudice began to appear. The N.C.C.J.'s earlier witness and effort was directed against that primitivism and chose, aptly, to concentrate on the humane basis. It came to be the most widely recognized representation of the brotherhood movement. Brotherhood weeks began to appear. Christians and Jews worked together on many civic and some religious projects. They united to fight back prejudice and the semantics of hate. Newspaper columnists, entertainment personalities were solicited for support so that they might contribute their reputations toward better understanding.

Almost inevitably a movement of this type begins to secrete an ideology, to summon a synthesis. At this point the older version of the N.C.C.J. began to come under suspicion, particularly from the more particular religious groups. Many Jews complained that the theoretical basis for intergroup understanding was taking on the coloration of the Christian majority's theories. More Christians countered by expressing a new uneasiness. To them it seemed as if the brotherhood movement was becoming a new religion, a sort of generalized Biblical theism which subtracted witness to Christ and thus—to the Christian—denigrated the Biblical witness itself. Coupled with these attacks on the theory of the N.C.C.J. came the inevitable criticisms of a movement that was aging and growing sterile, outliving its usefulness. By the end of the 1950's the Brotherhood movement—insofar as it seemed to express the idea "good will is enough"—was beginning to be parodied and smiled at.

To the credit of the leadership of the N.C.C.J. it must be pointed out that the Conference was a catalyst at regularizing the change between the two periods. By 1960 the old taboos against discussing anything controversial in the N.C.C.J. had fallen away. By 1962 the Conference had assumed leadership of the new attempt to improve the quality of the religious aspect of civil life. Aided by a grant from the Ford Foundation and under the leadership of Dr. Lewis Webster Jones and Rabbi Arthur Gilbert the Conference assembled the first of a series of institutes at which hard-core, hard-headed issues were opened and aired more frankly than before.

Despite the change in the national movement or movements, on less organized scales much faith persisted in the idea that if left to themselves Americans could work things out. In part this faith was born of an underlying Rousseauian strand in American primitivism. In part it related to the lay mystique in American anti-intellectual circles. This mystique is based on the argument that the expert produces the trouble. If only lawyers, theologians, psychologists, social planners would leave the citizens alone they would come to amiable agreements. Such an argument appeals particularly to those who urge that religious impulses serve best when they are most inchoate and ill defined, least gathered and articulate. Particularity, it is assumed, disrupts brotherhood and breeds intolerance.

Still another factor in the continued faith in good will by itself is the individualist strand in American life that attacks organized forces, especially in religion. The American Catholic would be a good neighbor were he not prodded into action by the bishops. The Protestant is really a fine fellow, but the more active he becomes at the local Methodist church the more he is impelled to express the imperial goals of world Methodism. My Jewish neighbor is all right so long as he blends into the environment and scenery but the moment he emerges and combines with others to practice his religion at the synagogue he starts making arrogant minority claims. Such an argument insists that neighbors, one at a time, can generate good will—which would be enough—but outside forces prevent their exerting and expressing the good will.

Such an argument, even if true, would not by itself be sufficiently compelling or satisfactory. One must deal with realities and prospects. The prospect is that great numbers of millions of Americans will choose to express their ultimate commitments at the expense of superficial assumptions concerning the national good. If they must choose, they will choose for organized religion over generalized attempts at engendering good will. Theologically they will be precommitted against Robinson Crusoe forms of religion and will seek expression in the religious community, "The Body of Christ," or some other corporate entity. To wait until everyone abandons institutional ties, resists institutional authority, and rejects theologies which call for fellowship and gathered expression is fruitless. Once again, something more durable must be sought.

In the eyes of many observers, however, the move beyond good will into a newer phase soon spent itself. No doubt many a person confronted with a book such as this may feel that the newer understanding of pluralism has prematurely hardened, become formal and unproductive. The authors share that suspicion and concern. The *first* word asserted at a time when the breakdown of the brotherhood movement became apparent was one which called for the necessity of "dialogue." Dialogue came to be the voguish word, accurate in intention, to describe the new and necessary step. While dialogue did not often actually occur (we have seen it dribbled into inconsequential successive monologues), it was aspired to. The assumptions behind the sort of Socratic quest for truth and civility were brilliantly argued in the latter 1950's.[3]

The climax of this transitional phase occurred at the World Affairs Center in New York, May 5 to May 9, 1958, when a Seminar on Religion in a Free Society was sponsored by the Fund for the Republic, Inc. The truly historical character of this meeting, which gathered the theoreticians (and many of the practical administrators) in the field of church-state relations, is already perceived. There ensued an intricate period in which dialogue came to be defined, pluralism to be understood. Campuses, laymen's groups, N.C.C.J. units, church

3. See the essays by John Courtney Murray, Reinhold Niebuhr, Walter J. Ong, Stringfellow Barr in *Religion in America*, edited by John Cogley (New York: Meridian, 1958).

councils, even legislative halls began to reflect the concern for "dialogue."[4]

So: it was agreed that we lived in a pluralist society and that dialogue was the first move to be made toward other elements by responsible participants in a free society. After this was asserted, what followed? We are not yet out of the largely sterile aftermath of the "dialogical" period. Again, no doubt many readers of this book will come to it expecting one more dialogue. A monsignor, a rabbi, a minister will—it is expected—engage in another three-way ritual fire dance. They will, to change the metaphor, play the unproductive little chess move in which each word, each phrase, each argument becomes a pawn and the goal is to score points. If the book turns out that way, it is not in the intention of the authors. The three of us on meeting instantly agreed that we have already had enough fire dances and too many chess games; that we already know we need dialogue and brotherly acceptance. What is now needed is an answer to the question: "Dialogue for what?" What is the substance of dialogue, what is its context and intention? What should it produce in a free society? Of course, the fulfillment of such expectations must be and will be modest in a book of this type and in the arguments of men of limited experience. But we believe that a

4. In *An American Dialogue* by Robert McAfee Brown and Gustave Weigel, S.J. (New York: Doubleday, 1960), two religious leaders articulated, to most dialogicians' satisfaction, a set of "ground rules":

1. Each partner must believe that the other is speaking in good faith;
2. Each partner must have a clear understanding of his own faith;
3. Each partner must strive for a clearer understanding of the faith of the other. This implies:
   a. his willingness to interpret the faith of the other in its best light rather than its worst; and
   b. a continual willingness to revise his understanding of the faith of the other.
4. Each partner must accept responsibility in humility and penitence for what his group has done, and is doing, to foster and perpetuate division.
5. Each partner must forthrightly face the issues which cause separation, as well as those which create solidarity.
6. Each partner must recognize that all that can be done with the dialogue is to offer it up to God.

(Quoted from a summary on page 32.)

third phase, beyond brotherhood, beyond dialogue, is necessary.

Now no longer should the accent be on mood and on ground rules but on events and happenings. It is at this point that the actual, practical concerns and goals of the religious groups in society must be stated, sought, and faced. Here the constitutional lawyer, the historian, the theologian have their say along with the pastor, priest, and rabbi or responsible member of their congregations. We write on the assumption that we must first speak out of and then *to* our own communities—in my instance, the Protestant. It is necessary to discuss a mode of understanding the Protestant past, a mode of thinking and acting based upon that understanding.

Such an understanding must move between or around two poles which I shall call *identity* and *meaningful exposure*. By "identity" I mean the here-unexamined assumption that the Protestant community has a validity in its existence, that its witness is useful and true. In other contexts it is important to examine that assumption and to ask about the long view of the Protestant episode or venture in Christian and Western history. For the sake of the present discussion this witness must only be asserted. To do so is not a meaningless and fruitless act in itself because it deals with the first reality of pluralist society: large numbers of people in the separate religious groups do believe and believe seriously the tenets of their faith. They support it generously. They engage in the ultimate risk in concurring with the claim that the faith holds final destiny at its center. Thus the Protestant believes that his evangelical Christianity is an important and permanent witness to God's saving activity and is thus true; that God's saving activity is oriented to a confused and errant world and is thus necessary. Preserving the identity of that witness *in some form or other* (but not necessarily in all current institutional forms) is thus one half of the aspect of Protestantism which is involved here.

The quest for identity and its self-preservation must always be countered or balanced or evaluated by another norm:

identity for what? How best can this identity, this person-hood, this collective representation fulfill one of its two major purposes: existing for the good of man and society, for sharing and spreading the justice and finally the love of God out in the world? This is the public test of true religion. In Christian witness, who seeks only to preserve the identity of his own life loses it; whoever loses his life "for Christ's sake" will find it.

Exposure without identity means the dissipation of mean-ingful religious energy. It amounts to a belief in everything which is soon watered down into a belief in nothing. Ex-posure without identity was the accidental by-product in the laymen's mind of a syncretistic brotherhood movement. Identity without exposure means the self-serving of religious energy. It amounts to a belief that self-preservation and self-seeking are the highest goals of religion. Identity without ex-posure was the accidental by-product in the laymen's mind of a particular dialogical movement or period. Not only the layman was afflicted, however: perhaps most of all the insti-tutional expert found himself pursuing one goal or the other exclusively. The first assumption asked religious groups only to yield ground, the second to hold it—however genteel may be the manners.

In speaking to the Protestant community and then, out of it, to the larger national community, one is conscious that in a "three-faith" approach the greater burden is his. Because of the Protestant majority and the longer Protestant hegemony, the greater weight of interpreting the American experience falls upon him rather than upon his Catholic brother and Jewish cousin. It is within Protestantism that change today represents greatest threat and occasions greatest apprehension. Here the advocate of change is most readily regarded with suspicion and the agent of change from without, regarded with defensiveness. Here the advocate of change is most readily tempted to impatience and to overstatement, too ready denial of the validities of the past.

In speaking to the Protestant community and then, out of

it, to the larger national community, one is self-conscious about the scope of what is undertaken. To discuss the religious factor in national life is not a peripheral concern in a free society. Religious and nonreligious people alike must concern themselves with at least the sociological weight of institutions which claim the loyalty of 64 percent of the populace. Within that 64 percent the Protestant is conscious that if Protestantism reaches self-understanding and meaningful action, a religious majority will be seeking the good of the City of Man.

The reader, as he brings even minimal expectations to the book, wants to know where the three spokesmen belong in the spectrum of their religious communities. It serves the reader ill if they are uncritical on the one hand or eccentric and not representative on the other. For myself, the relation to Protestantism could be stated as follows:

In a day of tortured self-examination among Protestants, accompanied by a hazard that the past be denied, I take a generally warm and positive attitude to the Protestant past. This is true of both its earlier episodes: the Colonial experience when Protestantism coupled with "rationalist" thought and a creative environment helped produce our institutions and the early national experience when America for the first time "became" Protestant in its committed religious majority and in developing the national ethos. In face of non-Protestant criticisms of this past, therefore, I assume some of the burden of defending the choices Protestants made *in the context of possibilities then open to them.* Of course, as with all historical understanding, this generally positive attitude is coupled with a generous admixture of criticism. But for the present purposes that critical attitude is not in need of expounding. For the reader this means that in speaking of Protestantism I am not discussing a disembodied, disincarnate, ideal spiritual force which frees me from the concrete instance. It is always frustrating in religious discussion to be told that a religious impulse has validity but it has not yet ever truly been seen; it exists only in pure form in an ideal world. No: Protestantism relishes in and involves itself with the complicated, finite, partial, and often unlovely visibles of human experience.

Just as the view of the Protestant past is a generally positive one, at least as emphatically do I join the company of those who argue that only in limited senses was the base of the earlier Protestant witness suitable as a model for today. Such an alliance is not eccentric; large segments of American Protestantism share in the quest for a new basis of understanding and serving a pluralist society. But not all do, and the reader should be aware that on these pages there is an always implied and sometimes explicit polemic against a broad strand of Protestantism. That strand appears to me to be defensive and thus erratically aggressive, concerned about the prerogatives and endowments, the holdings and the prestige, the good name and the occupied ground, the legal preeminence and moral superiority of any venture connected with Protestantism.

The Protestant institutional or cultural imperialist will not agree with what is here presented; nor will the Protestant institutional or cultural pessimist (who recalls "the good old days"). The Fundamentalist of an anticultural Pentecostal type will have interest in identity but not exposure. Those liberals who stress exposure at the expense of identity and look to Protestantism only to spend itself in order to infuse the culture will not be satisfied. On the most sophisticated level, I do not think that the Protestant "sacralist" (e.g., Bishop James Pike after the *Engel* vs. *Vitale* Supreme Court ruling) will be satisfied. But a broad stream of clergymen of all ages, but particularly of that generation shaped by exposure to pluralism, and a wide representation of emerging laymen do share the assumptions which I gather here around the poles of identity and meaningful, serving exposure.

Can Protestants find a position not subject only to the vagaries of the moment, the pragmatic decision of "the case before us"? Can they find positions which are theologically and historically valid, strategically productive? Will these

17

positions allow Protestants to be both faithful *and* free? That is the concern of an emerging generation after the breakdown of "mere" brotherhood, the impatience with the ground rules of dialogue. No one can be the self-appointed spokesman *for* the element in Protestantism which shares these concerns; many can venture to report and represent its interests and in that more modest sense this contribution is to be understood. Why do Protestants often act viscerally instead of with mind and heart in intergroup relations? What is their understanding of goals in a pluralist society? Is there anything in the Protestant witness that can be brought to bear to serve in the new period of tenseness and often open conflict? Those are our present concerns.

# II

Consensus and conflict: these are the poles around which the spiritual aspects of national life revolve. Without question, large elements of national experience can be viewed as part of a consensus. None of the major religions does or should insist on a monopoly of claim for goodness or for producing social justice. None of them dare claim a unique hold on democratic institutions. Each of them, whatever its view of the ultimate truth of its theological claims, ordinarily recognizes the partiality of its claims in the civil realm and each regularly refers to itself in terms somehow equivalent to the idea that it is *a* participant in the free society.

To hold together such a society and to make it productive, at least one thing must be agreed upon: the ground rules. Any number of participants on a religious scale are, in the American legal statement and ethical understanding, welcomed in the civil arena. They are welcomed equally. A ground rule of this type, to be durable, tends to attract to itself certain theoretical justifications and ceremonial undergirdings. Thus America does possess in very, very broad and unclear outline, a sort of substantiating theory. "We hold these truths to be

self-evident . . ." is the preface to a sequence of quasi-theological assertions. Whether all of the assertions stand up to
the most rigorous philosophical or empirical analysis is unimportant here: what is here to be stressed is that as a matter of
fact the courts and the people interpret themselves in broad
agreement with these theoretical statements. Sometimes the
development of an "American Creed," or a formal ideology
is urged but most Americans have had the good sense to resist
such articulation and to rely on a fruitful experience against
the background of an ill defined yet real consensus.

Consensus is not the only fact of American religious life. The
free and pluralist society is theoretically and practically made
up of persons and units which are, on varying scales and issues,
competitive and conflicting, disparate and disagreeing. When
disagreements occur, what should happen?

The brotherhood movement urged immediate covering up
of the issues in the name of the consensus and its values.

The dialogical period commended immediate talking-out of
the issues in the name of the identity of the separate groups
and their values.

What happens, what should happen today? Disagreements
may, first of all, issue in open conflict. In the nineteenth century such conflict was common but it took a different form.[5]
In that period conflict occurred in what we might call "raids"
from the strength of an existing majority community to the
center of a gathered minority community which was physically inside it (a convent, a ghetto). Viewed from the other
angle, conflict could be stimulated by all kinds of falsification
of claims concerning the world outside the experience of those
inside the convent or ghetto of the minority community. The
eruptions were often inflammatory in the literal sense of the
term; they were always ugly and relatively uncontrolled.
The breakdown of the diagrammatic, walled-in pattern before

5. See Ray Allen Billington, *The Protestant Crusade* (New York: Rinehart & Company, Inc., 1952) for a detailed account of one aspect of
conflict, Protestant *contra* Catholic in that period.

American pluralist life was exposed to view has brought a new type of conflict into the open.

Because conflict is less physically violent and seems to have less of a root in ignorance and false claim, the prevalence of conflict in intergroup relations is not often recognized. When *"it"* happens in a local community it is reckoned with as an isolated phenomenon. A battle over the Catholic church's stand on birth control in Connecticut or Massachusetts or Illinois; over a Protestant stand on gambling in Pennsylvania; over a Jewish concern about a nativity scene on a courthouse lawn in Connecticut or New York—these are regularly reported on but regarded as isolated, as exceptions. That good will is not enough, that Americans act viscerally in religious matters with some regularity is shockingly clear in the accounts of ten cities assembled by Eugene J. Lipman and Albert Vorspan. In their ten metropolitan instances disagreements issued in open conflict on a regular and disturbing scale of frequency and intensity.[6]

Religious disagreements, secondly, may be sublimated instead of issuing in open conflict. They can be postponed and ignored, minimized and neglected. They can be worked out in other ways. John J. Kane[7] has suggested with more than half-seriousness that in olden days Notre Dame football games provided one of these legitimizations of holy wars in the American milieu. Without question the whole spate of competitive "priest-rabbi-minister" jokes serve to take off some pressure in those communities and areas where priest, rabbi, and minister

6. See *A Tale of Ten Cities* (New York: Union of American Hebrew Congregations, 1962).
"Our ten studies of American cities demonstrate clearly that religious tensions and conflict are widespread in America today. Students of American history tell us that this is nothing new . . . From apathy to near-violence [conflicts] range, but there is one universal fact in today's America: Interreligious tension can no longer be concealed, can no longer be swept under the rug as un-American . . . there is serious interreligious tension which cannot be explained away only on the basis of increased publicity or greater public awareness. Careful analysis is required of the question: Why in a more mature America are interreligious conflicts apparently sharpening? And is this good or bad?" (pp. 292-93).
7. *Catholic-Protestant Conflicts in America* (Chicago: Regnery, 1955).

**20**

meet *only* in barroom-and-living-room-jokes. But sublimation and postponement of issues does not solve them and often builds up frustration. The hearty fraternalist who most lustily regales his brothers with tolerant priest-minister-rabbi jokes is often most nonfraternal when the claims of one of their communities might affect his pocketbook or his dream of America.

A third possibility is that disagreements may be resolved, or relatively relieved. This can occur by the defeat and capitulation of one participant or by new historical understanding and opportunities or by compromise. It is to the latter two of these hopes that today's experts in interfaith relations ordinarily strive.

Is all conflict necessarily bad, harmful, unproductive? Here, again contrary to the lay mystique of brotherhood as a sufficient basis for settlement, the American experience asserts something other. There are liabilities and there are assets to religious conflict, both in the religious and civic aspects.[8] Only if we understand the basis and meaning of conflict in religion can goals in interfaith relations be described. Without such understanding one would do well to return to a simple faith in emotive brotherhood or concentrate on sublimation.

Conflict, in Max Weber's definition, on a social scale involves a social relation in which activities are "oriented intentionally to carrying out the actor's own will against the resistance of the other party or parties." For a religious group to be the actor or agent in social conflict implies that it can assume the loyalty of a considerable number of people either for its institutional or religious goals. This in itself pays religion the compliment of at least not being only the acted upon, the adjusting element in a secular society. But the larger culture is precommitted to a view which judges religions in the moments of conflict and determines that conflict is contrary to religions' highest goals.

For one thing, religion exists in some senses to minimize con-

8. In what follows I shall make occasional reference to an as yet unprinted paper, *The Nature and Consequences of Social Conflict for Religious Groups,* which I delivered in a series on "The Church and Social Conflict" at San Francisco Theological Seminary, April 2, 1962.

flict for the individual and group, to protect them from all kinds of onslaught and assault on nerve ending and sensibility. Then why should it become the agent of conflict? it is argued. The larger society has a conservative expectation to extend to religious groups: it should be the protector of existing values, not an agent of conflict. The obvious evils of disruption and conflict in history (Crusades, Inquisitions) should call religious groups to penitence and not new conflict. Why cannot the religions all agree and produce a consensus, an overarching, all-encompassing religion of America? These are the questions which reveal how society looks to the minimizing of conflict.

The fact that religious groups in America *may* share large elements of the consensus, the inchoate American creed, and may overlap in many of their goals is no guarantee that contact will not lead to conflict. Social anthropologists in their study of early man observe that the further-apart species in zoological systems are less threats to each others' territory than are those which are near each other. The latter forage for the same food, fight for the same ground. So with the competitive elements in American religion, particularly within American Christianity. Their relative closeness to each other as species may accent conflict. The Protestant-Catholic competition for tax exemptions and perhaps even tax dollars is illustrative here.

Conflict may be rooted in nearness of species on limited ground; when it erupts (in the observation of Clyde Kluckholn) the antagonisms ordinarily are based on "one or more 'realistic' conflicts of interest *and* upon 'unrealistic' dislike."[9] One cannot always resolve realistic conflict without depriving members of one group or without unsatisfactory compromise. But, as the good will movements knew, one can readily face up to the "unrealistic" attitudes. Kluckholn's advice on this level has some merit for those who are too impatient, too "touchy" or "jumpy" in intergroup relations: "When it comes to large canvases, the social scientist would still do well to abide by

9. "Group Tensions" in *Culture and Behavior* (Glencoe: The Free Press, 1962), pp. 301ff.

what has proved a helpful rule in many medical cases: 'do nothing. Sit tight. Watch. Prepare for probable developments but do not interfere with natural forces making for recuperation until you are sure that action will be helpful or, as an absolute minimum, do no harm.' "

Sitting tight cannot be a permanent strategy on the level of realistic conflict, however. Competition of religious and institutional claims will remain and may even be stimulated as religions try to be true to some of their own stated goals. "I did not come to bring peace but a sword." Ideological opposition to all forms of conflict in religion will thus be not only unrealistic but untrue to particular religious witnesses, will contribute only to the relativistic, normless, unethical national Shinto.

At least these assets can be seen in conflict:

It is a tribute to the youth and energy of a religious group and a tribute to the intensity of conviction of a group; it contributes to nurture and definition; it provides opportunities for creative realignments that provide protection against worse conflict. (Thus the American Jew is better off in ripely pluralist America than he may have been in an America legally defined on Protestant or Christian terms.)

But conflict produces more liabilities. Annihilation, bloodshed, hatred are involved. Conflict produces the illusion of realistic reasons for difference between groups when actually there are few or none. "The denial by another of what I hold true, impairs my confidence in it" (Henry Sidgwick) and I act erratically and prolong the definition of difference. Reasons for separation from others must then be invented and no purpose is served. A variety of means for ending purposeless conflict present themselves. One is annihilation; another unconditional surrender; a third is coexistence, sometimes of a creative cast or type. The quest for consensus on legitimate levels and with legitimate means should be stressed. There is no particular virtue in the separation of elements which could agree, particularly in religion—as the ecumenical movement has set out to show.

Still other means for minimizing conflict include the passage of more accurate information from group to group. A surprising amount of misinformation and actual ignorance concerning claims is at the root of much social conflict in religious circles. Obsolete historical stereotypes are often used; conflicting participants often like to believe the worst about the others. Final movement beyond conflict, in Biblical witness, is eschatological; it belongs to the freedom and grace of God to bring this in. But "hope projected backward" calls man to minimize or channel conflict into creative patterns. Even a "tragic sense of life" would give a depth that the movement of "mere" brotherhood did not possess.

# III

Conflict between religious groups of the type that issues in visceral action can better be dealt with when its history, at least in the immediate context, is understood. I should like to delineate nine phases in the American development as a background. These phases overlap and often coexist but a basic historical progression is also involved chronologically. Americans may not be noted for thinking historically if by "historically" we mean in academically technical categories. Yet many actions in the religious realm can be recognized only when set in the context of the past. The national experience is not formed in the way a new recording is appropriated on the magnetic tape of a recording instrument: by erasing the previous band. Instead, it is like a palimpsest, one layer scribbled over another and from time to time earlier impressions are to be reread. This palimpsestic character accounts for various regional religious emphases. Much of what is written in this book about "pluralism" will hardly seem recognizable or urgent to the rural Protestant Southerner. He is basing his interpretation and action on an authentic strand of earlier American life, but one that has been scribbled over elsewhere.

The American experience begins with monopolist assumptions. The first explorers, of Catholic origin, began to work at the continent from the North in French Canada and from Southeast and Southwest, in the sections of the country which have become Florida and Southern California-New Mexico. No intention to found a pluralist society, no predestination toward dialogue was involved in this Catholic exploration. The Separatist-Puritan-Pilgrim strand which peopled much of today's New England with what we would call Congregational-Presbyterian religion is widely pictured as a movement for religious liberty. It was, but this religious liberty was pictured as liberty for the original colonizers who were edged out of England and were not at home in Holland. The dissenter could always be free—he was regularly reminded—to leave for "Rogue's Island" (Rhode Island). As late as the early years of the nineteenth century Yale President Timothy Dwight could picture the great wilderness and the forests of the western frontier as an eternal refuge for those who disagreed with the Congregational-Presbyterian establishment. By West he meant Vermont-New Hampshire.

Meanwhile from the south Anglicans populated and informed Virginia and the Carolinas, establishing the Episcopal form of worship officially. While this establishment was more relaxed and genial than the other two major types, it still was based on the monopolist assumption. Baptists and Quakers might be more free to worship, but they still paid their taxes for the Anglican establishment. The Middle Colonies, notably Pennsylvania but soon also New York-New Jersey and others, were to prefigure later attitudes which were eventually to help break down the monopolies.

The monopolistic assumption led to the second phase, which might be called pluralism but which was characterized by what social psychologists would call pluralistic ignorance. The seeds of change were present. Men in different regions of a uniting nation were worshiping in different ways. The nation was being formed as a loose federation of Colonies which united for practical reasons: issues of taxation, of military necessity.

It was not originally necessary for people forming such casual bonds to try to form a religious consensus or to determine terms of unity. An Anglican from Virginia and a Congregationalist from Connecticut could unite on civil and political issues and then go home from Philadelphia back to a way of life still kept intact. The few Catholics in the colonies in the Revolutionary period (some say 20,000 to 25,000) and the fewer Jews were so much seen as segregated colonies and minority emphases that they were hardly reckoned with by the rational religionists among the Founding Fathers. But they were there, organic and intact communities of belief. Failure to be aware of the meaning of their growth was to lead to later problems.

After monopoly and pluralistic ignorance came the time of initial contact and the beginning of disruption of the two earlier patterns. "Initial contact," be it noted, still occurs to jostle monopolies when the first Jews move into a Christian community, when the first Catholics move into a Protestant suburb, when urbanism extends its psychic hold to once-sheltered areas. These illustrations suggest once again how movement to a new level of relation does not erase previous ones.

"Initial contact" takes a variety of forms. What Georg Simmel calls "the sociology of the stranger" may usually be the first step. The intactness of community is threatened and challenged when the very first intruder makes his way into it. In early America this may have been the political stranger who represented federal concerns in the individual colonies (now states). In order to undergird and enforce the activity of the Thirteen Colonies he would present certain functional and administrative concerns. But he would embody other values than those held by the majority of the community. Even more than the political stranger who accidentally holds other religious views is the religious intruder. The Great Awakening (around and after 1734) effected considerable changes on this front in national life. Traveling evangelists would move from place to place stirring up religious interest. Their emphases would often differ from the local establishment. Their presence was threat and attraction, but always disruption. The stranger often unites the integral community over against himself. But the wholeness of his own moral experience, gained on a different pattern of ideologies from those of the larger community is a living witness to the partiality and incompleteness of the community's previous life.

Not only the stranger served and serves to disrupt monopolies. "Occupational gatekeepers" within the community occasion change. The professional and technical person in the community, trained outside it, as he carries on his bond with other communities on a technical base shares something of their life. Meanwhile, shaped by the larger experience, he is also turned in upon his original associations and carries over to them a transfer of his wider experience. The development of colleges and universities, the enlargement of experience implied by them, and the necessity to provide a Federal Government with people in each community who could carry on national affairs led to the development of more occupational gatekeepers and to change. Today, if a "local boy" returns from the State University and a metropolitan experience to engage in a more technical form of agriculture or shopkeeping, he brings back with him memories of and witness to the intact moral experiences of people from other communities which do not share the assumptions of the local majority.

More decisive than the stranger from without and the gatekeeper from within is the mobile person who carries elements of community from place to place. Colonial America provided relatively few occasions for a Catholic to move to Connecticut, a Congregationalist to Charleston. Colonial society was still largely agrarian and nontechnical. The effects of the Industrial Revolution, of immigration, of urbanization radically changed the picture. Protestant Massachusetts became, in the ninteenth century, Catholic Massachusetts. Immigrants from the Continent, both Catholic and Protestant, settling in the major

27

cities, overran the cities and their earlier assumptions. As a technical society moves one from place to place where his own technique is used and can be put to work (in war, in industry), he carries with him independent value systems which can be countered by those he newly faces. Unlike the immigrant, he does not move with his religious community and settle in parishes, wards, or ghettoes. He is a nomad, alone with his family.

Over three centuries of life on the North American continent had not served to prepare Americans for the nineteenth century experience of exposure and change. Initial contact led to the eruptions of conflict which came in the middle of the nineteenth century. Catholics, Jews, Continental Protestants alike shared the ugly experience and themselves often acted erratically and irresponsibly. To compare the treatment accorded Roger Williams and Anne Hutchinson, disrupters of Colonial New England, with the treatment accorded the Catholic in the years of "the Protestant Crusade" of Nativism and Know-Nothingism is not too apt or fruitful. The former were challenges to a legally established monopoly on the outsider's terms. The latter was in contradiction to the legally established religious liberty which should have guaranteed that there *be* no outsiders. True, the Protestant Crusade provides no really comparable tit for tat to the Catholic Inquisition, as later agitators might suggest. But the Crusade was a denial of the Constitutional assumption with its anticipation of liberty; the Inquisition had offered no promises that would lead to illusion and despair. The stranger, the gatekeeper, the nomad and particularly their hordes of immigrant brothers brought about an era of conflict.

Following upon these eruptions of conflict came a fifth phase, the attempts to pacify in terms of brotherhood. Good will, of course, was not born as a full-term child of the twentieth century. Men of good will in the nineteenth century worked to redress evils and bring about amity. But few of them sustained the inclusive vision of pluralism. So notable an irenicist as the liberal Horace Bushnell could, near the middle of the century, awaken public response equally to the three evils of slavery, infidelity, and Catholicism. If there were limits to the good will of the best individual men, the attempts to pacify were further limited by their slightly organized character. What was new about the twentieth century was the institutionalization and regularization of such impulses in organizations like the N.C.C.J.

When the limits of pacification on the basis of a superficial *esprit* were perceived, the totalist impulse began to appear. This impulse sought to devise a consensus or an ideology, a common faith of democratic values. The Common Faith (John Dewey's term) would either displace existing particular religions or it would be so much more dramatic that it would downstage the others to secondary character and interest. It would involve a celebration of democratic values; its liturgy would be nationalist in character; its established church, the public schools; its pantheon filled with the Founding Fathers. Thus Rabbi Charles Fleischer at the century's turn: "We of America are the 'peculiar people' consecrated to that 'mission' of realizing Democracy [which] is potentially a universal spiritual principle, aye, a religion. . . . Men like Washington, Samuel Adams, Jefferson, Lincoln [should be] placed literally in a calendar of saints to be reverenced by our future Americans as apostles of our Republic."

Fear lest this ideology be at the base of interfaith and brotherhood movements in their earlier stages led to widespread mistrust from the more credally oriented and liturgically based churches of America. It remains as an unofficial, perhaps *the* unofficially established, popular religion in America. Formal advocates and institutionalizers of the impulses have, however, been largely frustrated and discouraged. Reflective Americans, impatient with religious differences, at least do not want an invented national ideology to take the place of historic faiths.

If the last two cited instances suggest that the trend was entirely toward integration of national religious impulses into a harmonious whole, this was not actually the case. Undertones of suspicion and hostility remained; we must keep recalling that earlier experiences were not wholly or at least not nationally displaced. Calls for monopolies, for shelter, for limited contact, for conflict actually remained. But the twentieth century also saw some new forms of militancy which formally led to the breakdown of consensus and brotherhood. These were occasioned by new developments in church-state relations and in the sociology of religion.

Each of the major religious communities held some responsibility. Protestants, seeing their hegemony threatened, reacted often irresponsibly. Catholics, seeing their place under the sun enlarged, often were aggressive in preempting new areas of life. Jews, freed from ghetto existence, moved out of their communities and led to change in regions of Christian memory. New forms of conflict developed, now almost all of them on legal lines. This most recent form of conflict has led to the frequency of Supreme Court cases which test the meaning of the First Amendment. It is behind the Catholic interest in tax funds for parochial education. It is involved in every argument with Jew or secularist over Christian witness in public arenas. It is implied in the organizations such as Protestants and Other Americans United for Separation of Church and State or in the writings of a Paul Blanshard, the Catholic *Our Sunday Visitor* or the more blatant humanist organs.

Consensus also disintegrated through the apparent renewal of religious particularity. Various religious groups, fearing the suffocating embrace of American religious establishment in generalist terms, began to regather. Discipline, missionary life, theological clarity were called for. The generating center of the separate faiths was sought and appealed to at the expense of the overarching national faith. Thus the consensus has been disrupted both institutionally and theologically, both on tribal and on sophisticated levels. If good will activity was not enough, neither was good will theology—when it ran counter to the existing theologies.

The eighth stage, after the disruption of consensus, was the cluster of new attempts to promote civility. The years since World War II have seen a tremendous stir on this front. Foundations such as the Fund for the Republic, Inc., considered religious conflict so near the edge of barbarity in the era of realized pluralism that they saw the conflict as a threat to the survival of democratic process. "Religion in a Free Society" began to be understood on a new basis as a result of such efforts. Pluralism became a byword on campuses and at seminars; the N.C.C.J. redefined its interests. Conferences of various technical groups met to see what each could contribute. Thus for several years a "4 C's" conference has been held to discuss the role of the press. *Commentary, The Commonweal, The Christian Century* and Columbia University School of Journalism have met to iron out on Jewish, Catholic, Protestant, and nonmilitant secular grounds many problems and conflicts. ACURA, an Association for the Co-ordination of University Religious Affairs is typical of the organizations which try to deal with the perplexing problems of separated religions on tax-supported university campuses. The courts are more and more forced to work toward definitions which will lead to civil dialogue and new agreements, though their efforts will often mean immediate increase in conflict as steps toward later solutions.

No one could easily argue with the benefits which have accrued from such efforts. There are some by-products or side effects which must be recognized, however. Sometimes the celebration of the fact that pluralism is recognized, that dialogue is desired, itself becomes a quasi-religious impulse which can paralyze theological inquiry and the moral quest. If we can "get along with each other" this is taken to mean that we are the same as each other, and a formless, normless religion of pluralism begins to develop. Or again, a serious by-product of realized pluralism is the charter it gives individual religious communities to pursue their goals with a new sense of freedom. This freedom often leads to license, to the pursuit often of irrelevent individual goals at the expense of the common good.[10]

Concern with the danger lest realized pluralism become a charter for irresponsibility on the level of the common good has led to the most recent phase in interfaith understanding in America. So newly emergent is it, that it would be hazardous to try to capture it in a phrase. It is more fruitful to characterize certain aspects of it, and this whole book is an attempt to delineate some of the needed emphases today. At the heart of all the newest efforts is the question which concerns religious and national leaders today: Why, under the surface of gentility in America, is there an undertone of persistent religious strife; why is there so much *meaningless* conflict despite all efforts to come to terms with pluralist society and a Constitution that guarantees equality of religious opportunity?

Historical understanding and the study of social psychology will help in this phase, but will not suffice. Somehow consolidations of gains must be institutionalized. The religious

10. The best discussion to date on the subject of this "columnization" of national life on hardening and not always meaningful pluralist grounds is Gerhard Lenski's *The Religious Factor* (New York: Doubleday, 1961). See particularly Chapter Eight and its section "Drift toward compartmentalization?", pp. 326ff.

"It may well be that compartmentalization along socio-religious group lines is the best we can hope for in a society which is religiously divided as ours is, if at the same time we are to preserve the values linked with the various subgroups. However, if given the group loyalties of Americans, compartmentalization is the best arrangement we can achieve, it would seem desirable that this alternative be chosen *after rational exploration and consideration of the alternatives.* Currently we seem merely to be drifting into a type of social arrangement which Americans of all faiths might well reject if they became fully aware of all it entails.

"This problem should be of special concern to religious leaders. Our current drift toward a 'compartmentalized society' could easily produce a situation where individuals developed a heightened sense of religious group loyalty combined with a minimal sense of responsibility for those outside their own group. In a more compartmentalized society there is good reason to fear a weakening of the ethical and spiritual elements in religion and a heightening of the ever dangerous political elements. Such a development would be a serious departure from the basic ideals of all of the major faiths in America, sharing as they do in the Biblical tradition. Hence, on both religious and political grounds, Americans might do well to study more critically than they yet have the arguments advanced by advocates of pluralistic society."

groups are being called upon to rethink and restate their institutional goals. Without hardening into ideology, theories are necessary. Religious and nonreligious elements in society cannot *only* "play it by ear." So in the more recent efforts—such as the N.C.C.J.'s First Institute on the project Religious Freedom and Public Affairs—clarity of aims in the separate groups was sought. The hit-or-miss character, the inner contradictions, the failure to relate institutional goals to the common good in the religious groups have become apparent.

The religious and the nonreligious elements in society are being called to analyze on terms consistent with their histories and theologies: What is the present nature of American society? What do you hope for in society? What should you hope for in society, given both the concern for the validity of your own impulse (identity) and a concern for the whole civil body (meaningful exposure)? How did we come to have the kind of pluralist society we now have? Is the present situation of external concord, legal tension, and emotional reaction the best we can hope for? Can Americans better understand each other's interpretations of the religious heart of the City of Man? While others address themselves to secular or Catholic or Jewish answers to these and similar questions, I am assigned the task now of addressing them to Protestant elements and providing some provisional suggestions or answers from out of *a* Protestant context. This cannot be done by regarding Protestantism only as an entity born in 1517 but by seeing it in its own light as an enduring Christian witness.

# IV

A Protestant interpretation of faith and culture in America grows out of a Biblical witness which throws the Christian into responsible life in the world (Romans 13) and in a revolutionary relation to the world (Revelation 13). The Christian is asked to preserve the identity of witness to God's *eph hapax*, his once-for-all particular way of dealing with man in Jesus Christ. Man is ill served, the Protestant believes, by dissipation or dissolution of this witness in the development of national "common faiths." "There is none other name under heaven given among men, whereby we must be saved" (Acts 4:12).

The interest in Christian identity, a consistent Protestant concern, is never used, however—least of all by Jesus in gathering disciples—as a charter for turning one's back upon the civil good and on personal need. The parables of judgment preserved in the Gospels picture Jesus describing people being judged not for the ways they kept their credal intactness artic-ulate but for what they *did*, what they did for others. The development of a disciplined cell of followers was as much a concern of Jesus as was its polar contrast: the expending of the resources of the cells for the sake of the world. Even the parable which has a sort of doctrinal reference, the story of Dives and Lazarus ("They have Moses and the prophets; let them hear them") does not regard the revelation as an end in itself but judges the Rich Man for his misuse of the Scrip-tures to promote irresponsibility to the beggar at his gates. The self-serving institutionalism of Protestants who look *first* to the preservation of their good name, their status, their oc-cupied ground, their prerogatives and endowments, has no basis in the New Testament charters of church life.

Early Christianity also lived between the poles of identity and exposure. The "liberals," apologists such as Justin Martyr in the second century, sought to relate the Christian faith to the Old Testament and the contemporary culture without see-ing a diminution of specifically Christian witness. But even the more rigorous apologist—one thinks of Tertullian—who worked radically to preserve a Christian sense of identity in a syncretistic culture, refused to withdraw Christianity from all sense of involvement in the culture. "We pray, too, for the emperors, for their ministers and for all in authority, for the welfare of the world, for the prevalence of peace, for the delay of the final consummation" (Tertullian's *Apology*, c. 197).

The Second Century *Epistle* to Diognetus (c. 130-180) is often seen as an attempt to relate Christianity's sense of identity to the civil society. There is little here, too, of the self-serving institutionalism associated with so much of today's religion:

> For Christians cannot be distinguished from the rest of the human race by country or language or customs. They do not live in cities of their own; they do not use a peculiar form of speech; they do not follow an eccentric manner of life. . . . They live in their own countries, but only as aliens. They have a share in everything as citizens, and endure everything as foreigners. Every foreign land is their fatherland, and yet for them every fatherland is a foreign land. . . . They busy themselves on earth, but their citizenship is in heaven. They obey the established laws, but in their own lives they go far beyond what the laws require.

Admittedly, these are writings from a time when Christianity looks to survival and is not, therefore, tempted to press its claims.

The decisive reversal, which still motivates so much religious, Christian, and Protestant thought a century and a half after the formal legal dissolution of the emphasis, came with the Constantinian-Justinian settlements. In these legal conversions of the Roman Empire the Christian Church had its *imperium* in the world. On this ground, it did look to its name and status, its occupied ground, its prerogatives and endowments. In the process it built into the Christian *psyche* that attitude toward the state which is still reflected in every request for exemptions and favors for religion. In the Constantinian period (from 313 on) the emperor granted financial favors to African churches, exempted the clergy from political duties, convoked Synods for the church, passed and administered and enforced laws of the church. By 392 A.D. the emperor was prohibiting pagan worship as a crime (Codex Theodosianus, 16:10, 12.) It would seem strange to come into an interfaith gathering in the 1960's and assert that it can be understood only in the light of fourth and sixth century definitions. But whatever Christians do for a millennium and a half must, we may safely assume, have some bearing on their existing habits. The desire to enhance their "place under the sun" in the legal sphere is obvious even one hundred and fifty years after America's last trace of formal legal religious establishment! Any progress from the Protestant side in interfaith and church-state relations will have to begin with a historical and theological appraisal of the imperial remembrance in daily action.

That charter for that millennium and a half is best seen in St. Augustine's *City of God*. The Middle Ages were not, of course, a conscious constitutionalization of the Augustinian vision. We dare not picture pope and princes sitting down together at a church-state seminar and poring over the document as a plan for law and action. But the *City of God* was a sufficiently intuitive philosophy of history that it overarches many of the variants that developed during the next one thousand years. To many *The City of God* is an unambiguous testimony to Christian disinterest in the world, a witness to the irrelevance of secular history, a defense of the Christian place in imperial affairs. It is a testimony, but by no means an unambiguous one. Dr. John O'Meara[11] has recently developed Augustine's concept of a *natura* which belongs both in the City of God and the *civitas terrena*. A certain nature exists which can be used in common by both the City of God and the city of Man (or even the city of the Devil!). This nature is good in itself (XV.22); it takes the forms of institutions and activities and enters into everything except the wills of evil men.

> The things used in common, therefore, by the two great eternal and mystical cities are good, but limited and temporal. They do not constitute a third city, for the cities in question have to do with the wills of men and angels. These

11. *Charter of Christendom* (New York: Macmillan, 1961), pp. 46ff.

cities existed before earthly created nature and will exist when it is no more. In this earthly period, created nature is used by citizens of both cities who can share most things, with, however, the great exception of religion and worship: this is the great and significant divide.

It is significant that the second phase or episode in Christendom's millennium and a half, Protestantism, concentrated not on the Catholic interest in the First Article, of Creation (*natura*) but characteristically on the Second Article, of Redemption and man's justification. But when it regarded the positive good in the nonecclesiastical, the civil, and even the "secular" realm it opened possibilities similar to those implied in Augustine.

Thus the concept of *justitia civilis*, a civil righteousness which has nothing to do with the justification of man before God and everything to do with his right action in the affairs of man, serves as a bridge to the secular. Gustav Aulen[12] serves as Dr. O'Meara's Protestant counterpart on the basis of Protestant resources to decry any monopolistic intentions in the civil realm on the part of Christians and thus to undercut self-seeking institutional interests vis-à-vis the law and other religions. He, too, is concerned with identity and exposure:

> The settlement between Christianity and a secularized humanity cannot be arranged by constructing a communion where no communion exists, nor by concealing the possibilities of contact and co-operation that really exist. It is not allowed to reinterpret Christianity in order thus, as much as possible, to bring it nearer the secularized humanity. It is necessary to let everything be what it is. The difference ought not to be concealed. The difference is foremost a difference in the sphere of faith. The faith of a secularized humanity is—as far as it exists—quite another than the Christian faith, which is wholly a faith in the God who is the Father of our Lord Jesus Christ.

12. *Church, Law and Society* (New York: Scribner's, 1948), pp. 88ff.

The possibilities of contact and co-operation, on the other hand, lie in the plan of the Law. The decisive question is whether we can find any positive response for the Law claiming careful attention to "our neighbors." Such an attitude must be thankfully acknowledged wherever it is found.

Isn't it rather a strange idea that Christianity should have an interest in monopolizing the sense of justice and righteousness on its own account?

Then Aulen, with Augustine-O'Meara moves back to the Law of Creation:

Christianity has no interest in monopolizing tendencies. In fact, they are opposed to the Christian faith of creation and to the here-included conception of the Law as the universal Law of the Creator, a Law that, like the Law of the Creator, is primary also in relation to Christianity. Everybody who understands what the Law of the Creator really means must appreciate all endeavors towards a careful attention to one's neighbors and the human fellowship, whether these endeavors belong to confessing Christians or not.

Protestantism in its early institutional forms (German territorial churches, Calvin's Genevan theocracy, Scotland and Massachusetts Bay, Anglican establishment) may have operated with varying degrees of toleration, but at the heart of each was an extension of medieval Catholicism's monopolistic intent. This strand of Protestantism helped colonize America and, more important, even the Separatist and Dissenting strands in Protestantism when they came to America or took root here often insisted on the hegemony of evangelical Christianity. It is not without interest to note that the Southern Baptist, in legal terms a "radical separationist" on church-state affairs, will often be most concerned to define American national life on specifically Christian sacral lines (*vide*, common reaction to the Supreme Court decision on the Regents' Prayer in 1962). Normative Protestantism for the most part accepted the settlement of 1555, *cuius regio, eius religio*. The prince of the region determined the religion of the region. When the states were democratized, the majority—especially if it was Protestant or Christian—took over the prince's role. Prayer in the public schools should have a quasi-Christian and preferably quasi-Protestant cast. Assaults on this establishment by Jews or "secularists" were considered to be unjust.

If the left-wing or sectarian phase of the Protestant episode did not settle for establishments of religion, it did tend to establish communitarian emphases which again implied a totalist impulse, an interest in monopoly. Sectarian withdrawal, in other words, even more radically denied the potential of the *natura*, the fruit of *justitia civilis* as it turned its back upon non-Christian human concerns. Only eventually in certain Puritan 'Enlightened' strands (John Saltmarsh and his associates, for example) does a real rationale for the validity of the secular order and for other religious commitments come clear.

The resources of Augustine, the Reformers, the "Enlightened" Puritans were seldom drawn upon by American Protestants to legitimize the secular society and the claims of competing religious groups. The accent has been more on identity than serving exposure, more on institutional strength than on understanding and helping in the world. This accent may not determine all that Protestants do, but it has characterized Protestantism in the halls where Church-state affairs and interfaith impulses are discussed and is behind much of the "visceral" concern for religious self-preservation that is discussed throughout this book. Somehow one senses, long after the official end of the age of Constantine, a real fear among Christians including Protestants that the faith cannot persist without the shelter of an official culture, without the pretext of quasi-legal props.

The eccentric or one-sided Protestant interest in identity (on which Protestantism has no monopoly) in national affairs has been accented by the national memory of its imperium and by its not inconsiderable institutional strength. Especially in areas (South, mid-South, upper Midwest, rural America) where its institutions prevail, the temptation grows to seek monopolies, to press claims, to argue from strength, to be defensive about releasing any occupied ground.

Often unnoticed to substantiate the Protestant claim is an element in the formation of America and its national theology. I refer to the cultural good will shown Protestantism in American history in part because of the nature of the specific "Enlightenment" which informed it. Colonial Catholicism was small and needed hardly to be reckoned with; Judaism was even more insignificant; non-Biblical religions were almost unrepresented. The Founding Fathers, not notable for Christian particularity and often considered to be men of the Enlightenment, did not seem to fear "secularity," seemed to worship a God who served as a common reference to them, and looked on with a generally positive attitude though with some disinterest and unconcern at "the Protestant sects."

One can argue that the Founding Fathers and the basic documents (Declaration of Independence, Federal and State Constitutions, Bill of Rights) do not fully serve the nation in all its discontents because they did not actually anticipate the specific kind of pluralism that did develop in America.

What was the attitude of the Founding Fathers, the Benjamin Franklins and later the Thomas Jeffersons, George Washingtons, and James Madisons toward the religious groups? Madison, be it noted, was exceptional in that his "Enlightened" position was fused with distinctive Reformed Christianity in a synthesis that bears more study than has yet been accorded it. There were other exceptions. But the typical attitude could be described somewhat along these lines: the shapers of the documents behind the American ethos were generally reverent men. Their Christian reminiscence stands out most boldly when it is contrasted with the attitudes of French Revolutionary Enlightenment figures. They were in many respects conservative in their attitude toward the Christian deposit in the legal lore of the West. They were political men, mindful of the feelings and sentiments of a large Christian minority of the American people. They were theologically oriented (or at least deo-logically, if we keep the pervasive Deism of the era in mind). That is, in their minds there was no question but that the universe made sense, that a sense of order prevailed, and that man would be judged now or in the afterlife for his good and evil.

Thus references to "Nature's God," "The Supreme Being," "God" in general terms, drop with frequency and provide a counterpoint to their main themes. They had a respect for much in the Christian Scripture. They were given to making quasi-theological assertions ("We hold these truths to be self-evident . . . that all men . . . are endowed by their Creator . . .").

Negatively, they tended to be anticreedal, antidoctrinal, seeing the formalization of dogma throughout history as the font of intolerance and arrogance. They were united against "priestcraft" and all exploitation of religion through rites and ordinances they regarded to be magical or superstitious. But one grand theme pervaded all their work: men should be free, really free, to worship God as they chose. Therefore they tended to oppose religious establishments in which one must support another religion through his taxes. Gradually they worked toward legal disestablishment; in this battle Jefferson and Madison were leaders. They readily described man's fortunate situation as being one in which rational religion served to free and unite a nation.

Scratch the surface of the Fathers, however, and it is apparent that they had not yet reckoned with militant antitheisms; they did not envision the extent of secularity which is at the base of the modern world. Even more, they were rarely open to the claims of Catholicism; it was identified with foreign powers from which they were now freed. They had the luxury of welcoming Catholics in America because there were so few. But there seems little possibility in their writings that they would concur in a Catholic theologization of pluralism. (Madison's delight in "a multiplicity of sects"—the most Christian kind of assertion in the American Enlightenment—is far removed from John Courtney Murray's "pluralism is contrary to the will of God" in the context of the most Enlightened Catholicism.) They did not seem to envision a period in which Catholics could numerically or institutionally press their claims.

Now, vigorously, it must be insisted that these paragraphs are not an attempt to slip a justification for the Protestant *imperium* in through the back door, or to claim a Protestant monopoly in American institutional origins—I have good reasons for insisting that anything but this is the case. What I am asserting is this: when the Founding Fathers talked about God, religion in civil society, religious liberty, tolerance, disestablishment, they were not envisioning the kind of pluralism based on secularity and pluralism with large non-Protestant elements in it. Much of their genial tolerance for the particularities (peculiarities, Franklin called them) which marked the dogmatic-liturgical and thus to new irrelevant aspects of religion was based on the fact that they envisioned a rationally-eroded amiable Protestant basis for their Enlightened view. They were less secular than the European Enlightened men, and less theological than today's Protestant, Catholic, or often Jewish interpreter of their experience.

Appeals in today's conversations to the ideological base of American founding documents must therefore be tempered by a critical historical awareness of the limits of that tradition and by its subsequent transformations. But just as a moment ago in citing the nonsecular, non-Catholic-Jewish base of the American form of Enlightenment, now it becomes necessary to wrest the tradition (as promised a paragraph ago) from the Protestant imperialists who claim Franklin and Jefferson as their own.

Much of the defense of the "sacral" character of American official life made by Protestants in their attacks against a secularizing Supreme Court tries to identify the Founding

Fathers with Protestantism. But Professor Sidney E. Mead is correct, I think, when he criticizes those who base the term "post-Protestant America" on observations of change from the Founding Fathers as being inaccurate. America is post-Protestant not in the sense of departure from the founding documents but in the sense of departure from the nineteenth century ethos. America was not at birth so much as it became in adolescence, the nineteenth century, a Protestant empire.[13] Failure to note the deposit of Protestantism in the nation's nineteenth century ethos has led to frequent misinterpretations of the eighteenth century. Non-Protestants, in extricating the founders of America from the nineteenth century experience overdo their de-Protestantization of these figures. Protestants, reading the founders in the light of the nineteenth century, tend to overdo the particular Protestant character of emphases. America was shaped in a moment of vital fusion between genially rationalist thought, a generalized Protestant piety, and a fortunate practical situation. The moment of shaping is as informative to the student as it is unrepeatable to today's planner in church-state affairs. What is lacking in most religious study of the founding era is the recognition that the overtly secular character of today's pluralist life is *not* clearly anticipated in the Protestant Enlightenment this continent knew.

Thus the possibility of a new Protestant interpretation of the American experience will depend upon the ability with which Protestant historians, theologians, churchmen, and laymen can correlate exegesis of the founding documents with both a revealed secular-pluralism and a more particular evangelically Protestant witness. Such an interpretation is being born today in the writings, varied as they may appear, of men such as Winthrop Hudson, Franklin Littell, Peter Berger,

13. Winthrop Hudson, *American Protestantism* (Chicago: University of Chicago Press, 1961) makes this point in a clear fashion through an inversion of chapter title terms. Chapter I is "The Shaping of American Protestantism, 1607-1787"; Chapter II is "Shaping a Protestant America, 1787-1914"; and Chapter III is "Protestantism in Post-Protestant America, 1914—".

Dean M. Kelley, Roy Eckardt, William Lee Miller, Sidney E. Mead, Robert T. Handy and others whose names are preeminent in today's more fashionable bibliographies in this field. Some make their appeal to Roger Williams and others to James Madison; some stress the rationalist side of the experience and others the Protestant-pietist; some, the eighteenth century and others the nineteenth. But they are united in their scholarly assault on the Protestant hegemony; in their theological interest in Protestant witness; in their more open attitude toward secularity.[14]

# V

In today's Protestant interpretations, at least four lines contend for acceptance. (I am here referring only to the options that will make any sense outside Protestantism, and will not deal with the out-and-out visceral or nativist impulses which remain but which should not be taken too seriously.) The first line tends toward a "Catholic" interpretation of culture. Some Protestants, notably in the Anglican communion, share the kind of approach to the Christian past in the West which we associate with the name of Roman Catholic historian Christopher Dawson. Dawson, an amazingly informed and articulate giant in his field of research mourns and regrets the passing of Christendom, of a culture informed by the faith as a basis for Western life. The Protestants seldom anchor their view in a romantic notion of medieval history; they seldom model their approach after any specific historical manifestation (e.g., Carolingian times).

14. It is not without interest that the generation immediately preceding theirs tended to take a somewhat different attitude than did the majority of these who expressed support of the Supreme Court Regents' Prayer decision. In carefully guarded animadversions which should be seen in context, Reinhold Niebuhr, John C. Bennett, and James A. Pike disagreed with the decision and criticize its tendency to desacralize the American public institutions. The writers to whom I have just referred for the most part either can readily absorb the decision into their view of history or overtly and readily welcome it as an extrication from "establishment" thought. In the latter instance it is seen as a liberating factor for Protestantism and a clarifying factor for American institutions.

Ordinarily the Protestant-Catholic interpretation is more theological than historical. Anglicans such as James A. Pike and Norman Pittenger work through the doctrine of the Incarnation to stress how Christ informs culture. Bernard Meland,[15] while he has not chosen to discuss American life in detail in this context, effects a synthesis through a Christian interpretation of the scientific world view on liberal theological grounds. Paul Tillich (who asserts, be it remembered, with equal vigor the diastatic element as "The Protestant Principle") correlates Christ and culture through a Catholic essence which refuses to grant autonomy to the secular order. It is interesting that most of the thinkers whose theology can lead to a Catholic interpretation of culture have not ordinarily chosen to make quasi-Protestant claims for *American* culture on a historical basis and when they do they are quite effectively countered.[16] But to say that an approach to culture on Protestant grounds has little legitimate historical warrant in the American past does not say that it is untrue or impossible. We may very well need help from outside; the option dare not be lightly dismissed.

The second type of Protestant interpretation, supported by two disparate elements, effects a "secularistic" interpretation of the history and culture itself. I refer to Fundamentalism and "Modernism," the strange bedfellows which so often, despite contrary origins, seem to work toward similar goals; we found them together at the "Peale"-group meeting in Washington (see p. 5). The Fundamentalist or conservative interpreter nominally baptizes the culture as Protestant *or* abandons it as secular. But whether it is a J. Howard Pew asking the churches to be disinterested in concrete political and economic decision or a Pentecostalist turning his back on political and economic decision, the effect is the same: abdication of churchly responsibility in the secular order.

15. In *The Realities of Faith* (New York: Oxford, 1962).
16. The historical criticism of Bishop Pike's defense of the First Amendment on these terms by James H. Smylie in *The Christian Century*, Vol. 79, 13, 16-18, Oct. 31, 1962, impresses me as being largely convincing.

Protestant identity is kept at the expense of exposure. (I am aware that the "Fundamentalist" impulse calls for individualist Protestant witness in many public areas, but it has not faced up to the basic facts of modern cultural powers and modern corporate life, and interesting as it may be intrinsically, has nothing to do with the present topic.)

The corollary of the Fundamentalist abandonment of the public realm to the secularist is the "Modernist" secularization of the religious realm. The former promotes identity at the expense of exposure; the latter promotes exposure to the dissolution of identity. (I use the term "Modernism" here, antique as it may sound, to distinguish it from the more dialectically liberal influence cited in the "Catholic" category above and associated with names like Tillich, Meland, Pike.) The Modernist's heyday was half a century and more ago; Lyman Abbott's accommodationist sentence, "Evolution is God's way of doing things," typifies his successors in the political realm who assert that the democratic process is God's way of doing things and that God is not really to be seen as having a separate identity. Often this impulse comes from secular theology (an anomalous but not inapt term): thus Horace M. Kallen could write a book titled *Secularism Is the Will of God* on the orthodox Deweyite lines.

However, under Christian auspices much the same happens when Chaplain J. Paul Williams[17] calls for metaphysical sanctions and ceremonial reinforcement for a post-Christian democratic religion which would not aggressively supplant but would in effect render irrelevant specific churchly witness in the name of a consensus religion. It happens when Arnold J. Toynbee periodically calls for a universal religion in a world of crisis; when Deane Ferm in *The Christian Century* regularly points to a universalist road ahead in religion. In these instances great regard is held for the secular order which is

17. *What Americans Believe and How They Worship* (New York: Harper, 1952; 2d Ed., 1962). The last chapter in each occasions this comment.)

then religionized or spiritualized through some theological base or other.

The Catholic or pro-secular interpretations are countered by a third vision of the American setting, based on a warm regard for the large shadow still cast by Protestant institutions in the nation. Sometimes this comes as a defense of Protestantism in cultural terms (the Luce magazines, in their Christmas and Easter editorials—particularly in *Life*) are given to this; or as a defense of culture in Protestant terms (the Peale group, the writings of Dr. Edward L. Elson, formerly minister to President Eisenhower, and others). In these instances the genuinely great part the Protestant institutions held in shaping America is affirmed. As a logical follow-through, continued support of these institutions in culture and critique of other interpretations of culture, is urged as the best strategy in a secular time.

The fourth possibility is the cluster of emerging interpretations which are more "Protestant" than the first cluster, more synthetic than the Fundamentalist and more dialectical than the "Modernist," less self-seeking than the institutionalist. The theological justification for this option seems curious to anyone who has not followed the theological discussion of the past quarter century. Relying on British resources (via F. D. Maurice and others) it will speak of "holy worldliness"; via the Continent (especially Barth, Bonhoeffer) it criticizes religion in the interest of the Christian faith and witnesses to the Lordship of Christ in the middle of a world that has come of age (the latter thinker) or regards itself as having done so (the former, Barth). In America it may as readily rely on the theologians of the national experience, such as Abraham Lincoln.

In any case, the potency of "the world" is reckoned with and not denied or glossed over. There is no interest in a monopoly of social justice and political achievement in Christian terms. The Old Testament's earthiness is affirmed. The New Testament's accents on Christ's Lordship in a world that does not know him (Colossians 1, John 1, Ephesians 1, Romans 8) are pointed to, though not at the expense of the ongoing encounter with the demonic ("Love *not* the world") in the world of alienation from and hostility to God. It accents the kenotic, self-emptying activity of God in Jesus Christ. The Christian witness to God's work "in the form of a servant" is used to refute institutional self-defensiveness. Here Augustine's *natura*, Luther's *justitia civilis*, Calvin's concern for the body politic as a unit, the Puritan interest (Saltmarsh, again) in religious freedom, Roger Williams's "two realms," Maurice's "Kingship of Christ" and other resources are employed.

What all these views hold in common is this: a disinterest in monopoly and institutional self-interest; an interest in "identity" in a disciplined church which is in part separate *from* culture; an assertion of the Lordship of Christ in a secular world which leads to freedom *for* culture. On the other hand is an interest in "exposure" in a mobile, self-emptying church which assumes more, not less cultural responsibility than institutionally self-defensive churches take.

# VI

The attempt by a new generation of Protestants to do justice both to the secular potential in the public order and specifically in the American past and present as well as to distinctive evangelical Christianity has its parallels elsewhere. It recognizes kinship with those in the secular situation who refuse to develop integral secular*ism* as a closed system. The agnostic is more often this kind of Protestant's cousin than is the religious nationalist (in his fight against "atheistic communism"). Nationalism and Communism as creeds cannot tolerate agnosticism. But agnosticism is open to possibility and change. It regards with interest, often with reverent interest, the interpretations of political life and freedom which come from religious resource-centers.

Such an interpretation of Protestantism is at home with those who in Catholicism and Judaism ask *first*, "What is the common good?" and second, "How can I enhance my own institutional goals?" In other words, here as elsewhere, Protestant Christianity should have no interest in arrogating monopolies but only interest in the public good and with alliances wherever these are consistent with witness to God's Lordship.

Admittedly, the Catholic minority in the agrarian South has not yet seen much of this emphasis. Nor has the smaller Jewish community in the larger Protestant suburb, or the Catholic across the table from a P.O.A.U. lawyer. (Protestants also do not always see the counterparts to this view in secular-Catholic-Jewish communities!) A struggle, in other words, is going on within Protestantism. Ranged against the Protestant reinterpreters are a host of powers. Among them are the defenders of the Protestant *imperium*, the hegemonists who wish, wherever possible, still to legislate for Protestant claims and at least subtly to coerce minorities in a local community. From the other extreme are the iconoclasts who care nothing for Protestant history in America, who repudiate the nineteenth century without seeing the fruit of its moments of vital fusion (e.g., the theology of Abraham Lincoln).[18]

18. Winthrop Hudson, *The Great Tradition of the American Churches* (New York: Harper, 1953, especially p. 108) should be read by those who in Protestantism are embarrassed by its history and accept the myth that it had *only* imperial interests:

"The great significance of Lincoln is that he bears witness, in his person and in his faith, to the extent to which the free churches had shaped American culture. The true greatness of 'the great century' is that the culture that had been created could itself produce so great a Christian as Abraham Lincoln. The ideals, the convictions, the language, the customs, the institutions of society were so shot through with Christian presuppositions that the culture itself nurtured and nourished the Christian faith. So complete was the penetration of the culture that an Abraham Lincoln —lacking even a nominal formal relationship to a church—was enabled to reflect accurately and to exemplify profoundly the basic insights of the Christian faith."

Readers are advised to see this paragraph in Hudson's critical context to be assured that this is something other than romantic talk.

**49**

Neither the imperialists or iconoclasts are culturally so predominating, however, as the institutionalists who form the most effective barrier against a Protestant reinterpretation of culture which would be of aid to non-Protestants in quest of a common good. Institutionalists come in all theological shapes and forms and belong to denominations and inter-denominational agencies both small and large alike. I am not here speaking in inclusive terms which shrug off the necessity for staffing, supporting, or enlarging Protestant institutions in the country. (As a minister of a church, an editor of a magazine, a teacher at a university—each of them somehow or other a Protestant institution—I would certainly be a "double-minded" double-talking man were I to make this Docetic error!)

The marks of the institutionalist are clear. His view of church-state relations and interfaith conversation always begins with the question: How will this issue enhance *our* place in the world? His interest in the unredeemed world or the redeemed world that does not yet know its redemption is limited exclusively to seeing it as the place from which some are to be snatched and incorporated into his institution's life. His theology for the world is largely limited to public relations. His approach to other faiths' concerns in the public realm is basically *fiscal:* that is, he resents intrusions of religion into public affairs if it may cost him money (Federal Aid to other people's parochial education). His interpretation of the Protestant past stresses its good name for the sake of an attractive "image"; his interpretation of the Protestant present stresses its successes for the sake of a missionary "bandwagon effect": keep up appearances, do not quit while we are ahead, etc.

It would be Utopian to try to guarantee non-Protestants that this overpowering institutional concern will soon wane. As a matter of fact, the more threatened it is, the more assertive one can expect it to be. This is the source of what a discarded title for our book called the "visceral" interest in religion. Fighting off this form of imperialism unfortunately keeps Protestant reinterpreters from effectively criticizing and countering those movements in Catholicism, Judaism, and the secular order which deserve scrutiny. One cannot, therefore, guarantee the other conspirators in a free society that Protestant institutions will soon be self-critical and thus more open to interfaith conversation (any more than the alert Protestant expects a Utopian solution in other communities.) What *can* be guaranteed is that Protestantism today will present many voices, many faces, many options and that this is a protection for others. In this respect the Protestant-in-pluralism situation differs radically from the nineteenth century setting and its afterglow (almost to World War II) in which historian-theologian *and* institutionalist concurred for the most part in a definition of American life which would limit others. Stimulation of these differences by non-Protestants could be a productive activity!

To the degree that the postimperial view of Protestantism prevails, what changes will be effected in national life? Positively, one can foresee several immediate institutional effects. There would no doubt be a persistence of those forms of church life which promote "identity." That is, self-critical Protestantism which does not rely on a Protestant culture must be more disciplined, more informed, more sacrificial and thus —in Christian terms—more productive than will the self-enhancing form which wants laws and culture and ethos to do its work for it. The persistence of these churchly forms would come under more constant scrutiny and self-appraisal than did church life in the century of Protestant dominion.

There would also be some "negative" institutional effects. Protestants would here and there have to yield some ground in the legal readjustment, in the give-and-take of power relations. Their exemptions, their pet laws may be more critically reviewed in the future. In short, some risk is involved in any reappraisal and regrouping by one community inside a larger public in the name of that larger public's good. There is the risk of dissipation of identity in the name of exposure. The evangelical missionary impulse and distinctively Protestant motivation for service could be obscured by a general faith that Christian resources be expended in the larger society. Similarly, there is the risk of the disillusion with exposed life in the name of retaining identity as the frankly secular character of public life is revealed. That is, we do not yet know how strong Protestant Christianity is or would be if it had to rely on faith and not on culture. Would it dwindle to institutional minority and cultural irrelevance?

Risk there is, but necessary risk it must be, for at least three reasons. First is the practical situation. However expensive and inglorious "strategic retreat" may be for the moment and short range, for the long range it would be productive. The Christian who has faith in the truth and public utility of his witness must be prepared to let it stand on its intrinsic terms, even if its status may momentarily suffer. Second is the theological basis. *If* there is potential in secularity and validity to pluralism and if the Christian has nothing to fear in exposing his truth to other truths, then his truth calls him to that exposure. Third, in the long range there is a strategic necessity. In the current situation the pluralist-secular (or, for that matter, the Catholic and Jewish) interpretations of life each year are reckoned with more seriously in law and culture, entertainment and power relations. Each such reckoning forces Protestants to "yield ground" which they occupied. This progressive retreat can take on a pathetic and is taking on a defeatist character. The alternatives seem to be either a new imperial aggression (Constitutional amendments, use of the ballots) which would be contrary to theology and American democracy; continued retreat on existing ground rules; or recognition that—however worthy they may have been in the nineteenth century context—the ground rules have changed in the twentieth!

How is the more open interpretation which leaves the imperium behind to be affected? A multitude of answers and outlets appear immediately. It will not occur unless the historical and theological options are studied and consciously chosen. The alternative pictured here is not a "commonsense" observation any more than is any other element in the Christian call to discipleship and servanthood. All possible alternatives must be appraised constantly. I for one regard both the eighteenth and nineteenth century witnesses, incompatible as they are with what is called for today, to be largely salutary. This must also mean that today's answer may not be satisfactory in tomorrow's context.

Witness for this position is called for in Protestantdom through all outlets. Its intentions and substances are not often clearly understood by those it counters. Sometimes, one may suggest, it is deliberately misunderstood. Other times, one must ask, is it presented clearly and compatibly with the sincere Christian motivations of well meaning people? Those who have been told for three or four centuries that they serve God by staking out a claim for him in the legal domain in America can hardly be blamed for bewilderment when they find that today they are called to something different.

A corollary of this concern must be a Protestant empathy for alternative views. Why does the man at the conference table contend for something different than I do? Intra-Protestant dialogue is as important as is interfaith activity. The Protestant knows that it is worthwhile to anticipate problems. For instance, we can foresee that during the next decade the Supreme Court will be called on again and again to define the First Amendment. When the Regents' Prayer decision ruled out state-written prayers from the public schools it was obvious that the public had not been prepared by religious leaders. Hindsight tells us that once the instance reached the Court it was quite likely to eventuate in a decision of this character. Future rulings on Bible reading in the schools, Federal Aid to education, Sunday closing are in the offing. One cannot, if the courts base their decisions on cases and legal-historical experience, fortunately, anticipate the clear direction and detail of such rulings. But one can equip the religious public for life with both kinds of alternatives.

The Protestant may set an example in the public realm by self-discipline which will prevent him from pressing all his claims—including some equitable ones—as a means of limiting others' aggression. Protestants with ill grace criticize Catholics for seeking tax relief or Federal support for school loans if they themselves exploit every opportunity to press every exemption and look for every Federal gain they can for their own institutions.

I am afraid that Peter Berger speaks eloquently from within the Christian community for a suppressed sentiment widely held and rarely expressed by the dismissing outsider:[19]

> This writer has always been moved to irony when American Protestants visit Europe and express shock at the state-collected "church taxes" that still exist in some European countries. While it would be rather difficult to work this out in dollars-and-cents detail, the writer strongly suspects that the American state, by virtue of our tax-exemption laws, gives more economic support to the churches than European states in which religious establishments are still legally recognized. . . . A special irony attaches to recent Protestant outcries against Catholic attempts to milk the public treasuries a little beyond the point which everybody takes for granted. If we may allow ourselves a somewhat crude metaphor here, this is a case of people dwelling in tax-exempt parsonages throwing rocks at those traveling in tax-exempt parochial-school buses. It becomes especially ironical when we reflect that the clerical individuals who cry out against such use of tax money are often the only individuals in the community who themselves do not have to pay property taxes.

19. *The Noise of Solemn Assemblies* (New York: Doubleday, 1961, pp. 61ff.) Berger's book is frequently taken to be "iconoclastic" in the sense I described above. However, since his orientation is sociological and not historical it is hard to determine with what degree of affirmation he regards valid Protestant deposits in the national legacy. Perhaps he, too, feels that "the fathers" creatively related to their contexts in the past. He has little use for the present quasi-Protestant and generally religious national establishments.

For Protestants not to press claims may call for corollary self-restraint from other groups. Perhaps Catholics should take a realistic look at institutions other than parochial elementary schools to do more for training the children; a positive attitude toward "secularity" in education is beginning to appear in some Catholic thinkers. The Catholic can make some eloquent arguments that his schools do contribute to the common good; he has not done what he might to illustrate this to the non-Catholic.

The Jewish parent is understandably concerned over the vestiges of Christian piety which might be beamed his child's way in public educational programs. I can empathize with that concern, picturing my child as a Christian in a community of Jewish majority. Admittedly the child is placed in a bewildering crisscross of value systems. Admittedly such Christian rites may very well have no rightful place on public premises. But all of life in a pluralist society takes on some of that bewildering complex, and the Jewish parent who immediately presses for his rightful claims with no regard at all for the historical complexity often alienates his neighbors and may make it harder for Protestants who feel as he does to accomplish their work of reinterpretation. In these two cases I am dealing with general pictures. Particular and concrete situations must be dealt with on their own terms.

Similarly the nonbeliever in Christianity or Judaism may do well tactically to be patient with the larger community when it pays lip service to Christianity in the public domain. Were I a secularist who wanted to see the demise of religion I think I would not tamper with America's public religion. The Regents' Prayer in New York, in all respects really addressed not to God but "To Whom It May Concern," may very well be an effective enemy of true religion! Be that as it may, however rightful the movement toward the Supreme Court in this instance, it may not be productive if the principle were absolutized and pressed on all fronts at all times with equal vigor. Doctrinaire solutions somehow are uncongenial to the American resolution.

Throughout this chapter we have stood between the concerns for particularity and identity in Christian witness on one hand and exposure for service on the other. Here, too, no doctrinaire solutions were evident. The generally salutary character of the American experience must be recognized even by the more impatient. This continent, the "New World," offered a new situation for man. Inevitably there would be change, false starts, misunderstandings, conflicts. The oil-and-water mix of continued religious witness in a continent colonized in an era in part "post-Christian" would naturally cause confusion. We cannot hope to settle in this book or in our generation the questions concerning the extent of consensus a society needs for lubrication and glue, the extent of self-nurture a particular religious community needs to carry on its mission. Lenski's question remains: should pluralism and columnization be stressed or should the accent fall on national "spiritual" unity? It, too, admits of no doctrinaire solution. But it calls for self-conscious solutions, in each practical instance. The decisive question is: Pluralism for what? Identity for whom? If one looks only to the self-identity of religious institutions this drains and saps society and contradicts Protestant witness to the Lordship of Christ.

If one looks to identity as a resource-center for nurture, propagation, and service, all is seen in a different light.

# VII

A final word must be spoken against a messianism or Utopianism which is often voiced in the circles of good will. No one can keep his sanity in interfaith or church-state relations unless he has—I hope the repetition of the phrase does not make it hackneyed today—a "tragic sense of life." That is, no matter how open to transcendence of history a faith may be, its incarnation in institutions is necessary. Since insti-

**56**

tutions are collective representations, they have an essentially political nature. Since numbers of these collective representations exist in a free society, their relations to each other will be essentially political.

If politics is implied, then along with it one must recognize compromise and concession, aggression and withdrawal. No one can have everything the way he wants it all the time and not everyone can have anything the way he wants it much of the time at all. The Christian Scientist is frustrated in his attitude toward healing whenever the community around him fluoridates water. The Jehovah's Witness stands by in fury as the community takes his child and transfuses blood into him to save a life. The Mormon knows his grandfather had to adapt and forego some religious practices which ran counter to the laws and mores of the community. The Catholic pays for a double system of schooling. The Jew sees his child perplexed at the Christian witness in a community of Christian majority. The Protestant is disappointed that he cannot exercise his religious interests in the public sphere where a tiny minority objects. All together wish that the world had unity and peace, that Russia would be converted and lay down its weapons and that Everyone Would Live Happily After.

To assert that not all will come out right in the end is not a profound assertion nor is it a license to neglect the quest for justice. But strangely in the religious sphere, where less optimism about the empirics of history is anticipated on a doctrinal basis than it might be elsewhere, the tragic sense of political limitation is often forgotten. Without question, the visceral reaction to religious conflict is prevalent wherever frustration at the limited and political nature of decision is recognized. The whole man, the educated and reasonable man, knows from history and observation that not all he wishes to see prevail will prevail, at least not immediately.

Steeled by such a sense of limitation, he could take courage by some of the reappraisal of religious liberty being undertaken today. He can take comfort from the competition within the religious clusters. However America thinks denominationally (over 250 varieties), it thinks sociologically in four-way categories: Protestant, Catholic, Jew, secular (or some other such name). The protestations of Orthodoxy, High Anglicanism, and other voices to the contrary, this is how the configurations of life appear practically. In the four-way view, he no longer relies on Madison's faith in "a multiplicity of sects" so he should stimulate differences within them for his own protection. We know that Protestants are divided between those who desire a Protestant America and those who recognize a pluralist one; that Catholics are divided as to how positively they should regard the pluralist experience; that Jews sometimes stress the religious, sometimes the secular character of their community and its alliances. The "outsider" to any of these communities is naïve when he calls for unanimity and monolithicity within any of the four. He does best to hope for continued intracommunity conversation and dissent.

He can look at the historical background and the current setting of the faiths and see inconsistencies and embarrassments. What about Catholics in Spain and Columbia? What about Protestant professions of religious liberty and their own record in New England two centuries ago? What about Jews in Israel, where they have their only opportunity to govern a nation and do so without the American definition of religious liberty embraced by American Jews? What about them? The historical argument again offers safety to the "outsiders."

How is that each religious group has a blind spot? Does not the secularist know that abolishing Biblical religion from the schools does not necessarily lead to neutrality but actually to the elevation of Secularism or—worse—Nationalism to religious ultimacy? Protestants and Jews accuse Catholics of imposing their views of morality on the community in matters of birth-control legislation; Protestants are beset by Catholics and Jews for trying to do the same in antigambling measures; Jews, by Catholics and Protestants on the matter of Sunday closing. Can't they see their inconsistency? No, in each instance each community exempts itself. Again, there is protection in this intercommunity scrutiny and criticism.

These issues will increase, not decrease as the inclusive federal-national character of American decision enlarges. But even in the enlargement of issues to billboard size there is a protection unknown when it existed only in fine print and footnotes. A local community or region may have a disturbance which does not interrupt the nation and other regions. But the experience may be suffocating for minorities in the area. In an age of mass communications, a strong Federal government, a sort of welfare state, news travels fast and issues are rendered macroscopic.

The broader the base, therefore, the more apparent noise and ugliness in religious conflict. But the broader the base and the more the publicity, the more likely it is that competing and disparate elements be taken into consideration and a more political compromise be effected for protection. But the theoretical counterpart to this protection is disturbing. More and more it is apparent that Americans are abdicating to courts and schools, to the public arena, the task of solving religious problems.

In *The Great Tradition of the American Churches* Winthrop Hudson complained that Americans were more and more expecting "the state" to do what "the churches" were failing to do in the line of teaching. This reflected an impatience with the voluntary tradition and the separation of church and state. Today one could go further: the development of pluralism from a ground rule of national life to a descriptive basis for its consensus is dangerous. Pluralism is a ground rule and not an altar. One cannot cancel out moral and theological seriousness because Americans have been revealed to be able to get along civilly with many different religions. Public utility is not the only question to be asked of a generalized religiousness.

Today in schools, on campuses, at interfaith gatherings,

the celebration of the fact that we get along reasonably in a pluralist society is so fervent that it is often unrecognized that "pluralism" is insubstantial, is devoid of content. When it is recognized, the desire grows that it be given a content, a consensus-morality or religion. More and more the churches seem to want the pluralist society to do what they fail to do individually and ecclesiastically. They want it to be productive of values, want it to be the teacher. Now that the walls of ghettoes are broken down, and society is more interactive, fears grow that one may lose his identity. Therefore he expects a national consensus to provide an identity; he wants this to be propagated in the schools without offending existing religions. Too much weight is being placed on the part of elementary education in society. It cannot bear the ideological strain. Must public institutions fill the gap left by parents, churches, and synagogues which fail to complete their missions of nurture?

If pluralism does not become the base for an ideology, American religions will be in their best positions. Assets abound. The good will to which we referred on the first page can be counted on a long way. The positive regard with which the American experience is held can be drawn upon. Ideologies and fanaticisms can be resisted, for the sake of maneuverability and political opportunity.

Such patient regard for the other *and* his history *and* his ideas goes beyond the good will which proved to be deficient when tested. A divine potentiality in the secular unfolding of history is being newly regarded by churchmen who have called for a more disciplined church life. Such a setting permits one to keep his eye on the City of God, which has foundations, while he learns real temporality in the City of Man, which needs foundations. The double vision, the Protestant believes, is his own best contribution to a first, best hope of earth.

# A CATHOLIC
# VIEW
# OF CONTEMPORARY
# CONFLICT

**by Joseph N. Moody**

In man's recorded past, there is little that can compare to the planting and growth of the American community. Our history from its earliest beginnings has a romantic appeal which attracts the literate in most areas of the world. Those who consider themselves enslaved have responded to the story of our emerging liberties. The backward have sought to imitate our technological advance. The weak are jealous of our power. Behind all these is an American dream which has provided the motive power for much of our achievement. No serious historian would question the contribution of the religious groups to the formulation of this vision of America.[1]

The American Catholic belongs in the mainstream of this success story. Catholics played an important role in the period of discovery and exploration, as so many of our place names

---

1.   Thomas C. Hall. *Religious Background of American Culture* (Boston: Little, Brown & Co., 1930).

suggest. But the adventures of pathfinders and missionaries were largely outside the English settlements on the Atlantic seaboard which were the seedbed of our nation. It was in these that a new people was being formed with Catholics as a minuscule minority. During the colonial period it was only in Maryland and Pennsylvania that they were numerous enough, and free enough from penal law, to form an organized community. In Maryland they contributed to our later development by an Act of Toleration (1649), an important though limited gesture that owed something to their precarious position in the one colony in which they had been influential.

Though the Catholic minority was small and generally persecuted, it contained individuals of sufficient social standing to contribute to the forming of the nation. One Catholic signed the Declaration of Independence, several were in positions of leadership in the revolutionary struggle, two affixed their names to the Constitution and participated in the First Congress which added Ten Amendments. Most of the 30,000 Catholics welcomed these events, of which they were one of the principal beneficiaries. For the Revolution not only freed Catholics from legal disabilities; it made possible the formation of an organized Catholic Church in the United States.

This Anglo-American core, soon to be reinforced by refugees from revolutionary France, left an important heritage to American Catholicism.[2] Their writings reveal that they felt fully at home in the American scene. Their enthusiasm for the new situation erased the memory of discrimination—an unusual feat in any minority group. Their leaders circulated easily among the elite of the new nation. There was little consciousness among them that their Catholicism would be an obstacle to full participation in American life. They shared the buoyant optimism of their contemporaries in the future of their country and their own prestige was fortified by a

2. Thomas T. McAvoy, "The Catholic Church in the United States", in *The Catholic Church in World Affairs* (Notre Dame: Notre Dame University Press, 1954); McAvoy, "The Formation of the Catholic Minority in the United States, 1820-1860", *The Review of Politics*, Vol. X, No. 1, Jan. 1948.

steady trickle of converts of old American stock. Their acceptability to the Protestant majority was enhanced by their acceptance of the English Catholic pattern of reserve in matters that might cause conflict.

The original Catholic minority bequeathed to their successors a pattern of acceptance of the political and cultural structure of the United States. This pattern would be strained by the mass immigration that followed, but never destroyed. It would be intriguing to follow this trend through the stormy decades ahead, to note its strength among the "Americanizers" at the end of the century,[3] and to weigh its influence today among Catholics who are attracted to journals such as *Commonweal*. Such an inquiry might be more useful than the adoption of the categories "liberal" and "conservative" which often obscure the complex reality.

In addition to acting as a leaven among the immigrants and providing leaders for several decades,[4] the Anglo-Americans succeeded in establishing a church structure among the scattered Catholics in the new republic. This was the work of its first bishop, John Carroll, a native-born Marylander, whose see at Baltimore was officially erected in 1789 and embraced the entire territory of the United States. He was a friend of Franklin and other leaders of the emerging nation and followed with interest the efforts to write a Constitution. While the project was still a dream, he wrote to an English friend on February 27, 1785:

> We had all smarted heretofore under the lash of an established church, and shall therefore be on our guard against every approach to it.[5]

3. Robert D. Cross, *The Emergence of Liberal Catholicism in America* (Cambridge: Harvard University Press, 1958).
4. The story of American Catholicism can best be followed in the biographies of its leaders, as the best work in this still scantily cultivated field has been done in this area. For an example of a later Anglo-American leader, see John Tracy Ellis, *John Lancaster Spaulding*, (Milwaukee: Bruce Publishing Co., 1961).
5. John Tracy Ellis, "Church and State: An American Catholic Tradition," in *Harper's*, Nov. 1953, p. 64.

*A Catholic View of Contemporary Conflict*

Shortly after the Convention had completed its work, he gave his public approval in the *Columbian Magazine* of December, 1787:

> Thanks to genuine spirit and Christianity, the United States have banished intolerance from their system of government, and many of them have done the justice to every denomination of Christians, which ought to have been done to them all, of placing them on the same footing of citizenship, and conferring an equal right of participation in national privileges. Freedom and independence, acquired by the united efforts, and cemented by the mingled blood of Protestant and Catholic fellow-citizens, should be equally enjoyed by all.

Carroll's desire to find a place for Catholicism in a country overwhelmingly Protestant led him, among other things, to favor a vernacular liturgy. Yet he was unswervingly loyal to the doctrinal basis and very conscious of the need for unity with the universal Church as represented by the Holy See. This flexibility on political and social matters, and openness on questions of pastoral concern, along with strict orthodoxy and devotion to Rome, were to remain the dominant trait of American Catholicism.

The success of these initial efforts was recognized by Tocqueville during his tour of the United States in 1831-1832.[6] Scholars who have sifted his material carefully have disputed some of his data and his explanations, but it is agreed that he was the most acute analyst of the America he had observed. He found that Catholics had swelled to more than a million through natural increase, converts, and a growing immigration. He found them most fervent in the practice of their religion, and at the same time "the most republican and most democratic class in the United States." Coming from France, this surprised him at first. He found the reason in their

6. *Democracy in America*, two vols., trans. by Henry Reeve, ed. Henry S. Commager (N.Y.: Oxford University Press, 1947). Tocqueville published his first volume in 1835, his second in 1840.

64

poverty and minority condition: "All rights must be respected in order to insure to them the free exercise of their own privileges." He also felt that "no class of men are more naturally disposed to transfer the doctrine of equality of condition into the political world."

Tocqueville found no difference in the attitude of the clergy:

> The Catholic clergy of the United States have never attempted to oppose this tendency [toward freedom]; but they seek rather to justify it. . . . Thus the Catholics in the United States are at the same time the most submissive believers and the most independent citizens.

He was impressed by an invocation at a fund-raising meeting for the Polish people who were in revolt against the Czar. The priest, in clerical attire prayed:

> "O Lord, pitifully look down upon an heroic nation which is even now struggling as we did in the former time, and for the same rights. Thou, who didst create man in the same image, let not tyranny mar Thy work and establish inequality upon earth. Almighty God, do Thou watch over the destiny of the Poles, and make them worthy to be free. . . ."

Tocqueville noted that in America the government was religious though it did not favor any one creed. The result is "that there is no country in the world where the Christian religion retains a greater influence over the souls of men than in America." He finds that men's conduct, particularly in marriage and the family, is deeply marked by religious influence and that its usefulness to society is recognized by all. He believes that religion is indispensable to the form of government he is examining in America: "Despotism may govern without faith, but liberty cannot," for "the moral tie must be strengthened in proportion as the political tie is relaxed." "And I am inclined to believe that if faith be wanting in man, he must be subject; and if he be free, he must believe."

Both the country and religion profit by the freedom of religion and the benevolent attitude of government. The Catholic minority gain most obviously:

> America is the most democratic country in the world, and it is at the same time the country in which the Roman Catholic religion makes the most progress.

Tocqueville described the status of Catholics in America on the eve of decisive change. Their adaptation to environment which he stressed was an achievement of Carroll's generation. As the first bishop labored to relate Catholics to American life, he stretched his resources in clergy and funds to provide a skeleton for growth. He established bishoprics along the Atlantic coast—thus raising his see to the status of an archbishopric—and he sent pioneer priests across the Appalachians to the new settlements in Kentucky.[7] Carroll shared the vision of many of his contemporaries that the new nation was destined to expand westward and would ultimately span the continent. The establishment of a see at Bardstown, Kentucky (1808), indicated that Catholicism would move with the frontier and not remain geographically isolated on the coast. But the most strenuous efforts could not ensure the presence of the Church in all areas of the nation. Large pockets of rural America were not reached by Catholic missionary activity and little progress was made in establishing nuclei in the socially uncongenial South.[8]

This spirit of accommodation and this rudimentary structure were subjected to stern testing when the tide of Catholic immigration became a flood in the 1830's. American Catholi-

7. Among the earliest was the first priest to be ordained in the United States, Steven Bazin. Four months after his ordination in Baltimore in 1793, he walked to Pittsburgh to work along the Ohio. He is buried on the grounds of Notre Dame University.
8. The story of the pioneering bishop in the Southeast is found in Peter Guilday, *The Life and Times of John England, First Bishop of Charleston, 1786-1842* (New York: America Press, 1927).

cism was shaped by many factors, but the most unmistakable was its need to accommodate successive waves of Europe's poor. Unlike the Jews, who were generally from urban backgrounds and possessed some skills that could be adapted to city life in the New World, the overwhelming majority of Catholic immigrants came from peasant societies. Generally they were without technical capacity. Some were illiterate; others had a simple education.[9] Except for the Irish, they suffered from the handicap of language. All were regarded by the English speaking majority as foreign in customs and religion. The image of Catholicism in the Protestant mind as an alien organization was as much cultural as religious.

This impression was strengthened by their tendency to remain together to preserve their customs and their faith. A minority of them, mostly Germans with some Central Europeans, went to the West and acquired farms. Even these tended to settle in areas where they could retain contact with each other. But the vast majority carried bitter memories of rural life and were without sufficient funds to homestead. These were dumped in the expanding urban concentrations or found work on the transportation net that was pushing West. The coincidence of growing urbanization and large-scale immigration identified the newcomer with slums and unwholesome living conditions. It also aroused the hostility of workingmen of older stock who felt their status threatened.

These factors combined to produce the intense Nativist prejudice that left its mark on the Catholic immigrant.[10] Along with the political and religious freedom, which made his new life attractive, went serious social hostility which repulsed his efforts to find his place in America and which reinforced his tendency to the ghetto. It was a serious obstacle to his social mobility. Few among the Catholic arrivals made

9. The most notable exceptions were the German refugees from the revolutions of 1848 and the *Kulturkampf*.
10. Ray Allen Billington, *The Protestant Crusade, 1800-1860* (New York: Macmillan, 1938). Albert C. Dieffenbach, *Religious Liberty: The Great American Illusion* (New York: Morrow, 1927).

any noticeable ascent in the first generation and for most the handicap persisted into the second and beyond. Even today Catholics have the heaviest concentration in the lowest socio-economic class, 67 percent, compared to 53 percent of the Protestants and 46 percent of the Jews. But though poor initial equipment and social resistance retarded the economic advance of the Catholic immigrant, his urbanization placed him, along with the Jew, in the strategic center of American expansion.[11]

As a consequence of their position in the American scale, Catholics became prominent in the nascent labor movement and provided at least half of its members and leadership. Their influence within it may well have been decisive in giving the American movement its distinctive nonideological and pragmatic attitude.[12] Elsewhere the immigrants' concentration provided them with openings in local politics. As with the Negro today, the first step upward for the Catholic was apt to be in the lower rungs of the civil service—the Irish policeman became a folk figure—where he could find a position of some security and prestige without having to face the hostility of dominant groups.

His lack of training and external resistance combined to make the upward climb of the Catholic immigrant painful and slow.[13] He learned that education was the golden key to improved status, but found the religious climate at the better institutions uninviting and entrance difficult. Impelled to establish his own schools, it took time before these could compete academically with the existing colleges. While many of these newcomers came from countries with a strong artistic tradition, those arriving in the United States generally came

11. Eighty percent of contemporary Catholics live in urban areas, compared with 96 percent of the Jews and 60 percent of the Protestants.
12. This thesis is persuasively argued by Marc Karson, *American Labor Unions and Politics* (Carbondale: Southern Illinois University Press, 1958). For the decisive period, see Henry J. Browne, *The Catholic Church and the Knights of Labor* (Washington: Catholic University Press, 1949).
13. Well described in Oscar Handlin, *Boston's Immigrants, 1790-1865* (Cambridge: Harvard University Press, 1941).

from social groups which had little access to it. Hence they built and decorated their churches according to the prevailing norms of the Irish, German, Italian and Slav countryside—which were often low indeed. Only in music were one group, the Italians, in a position to make a positive contribution in the early generations.

Each of the national groups made their distinctive contribution to American Catholicism. The easiest to identify came from the Irish who provided a growing proportion of the clerical leadership and who acted as a bridge between American culture and immigrants of other nationalities. It was they who labored most consistently to prevent the fragmentation of the Church along national lines. As language made it easier for them to enter politics and qualify for church leadership, their abhorrence of the English dominance of their homeland prepared them for an enthusiastic acceptance of American political freedom. But while the Irish Catholics identified themselves thoroughly with the American tradition, they responded aggressively to social and religious prejudice. This truculence did not endear them to the older Anglo-American leadership.[14]

Other national groups tended to be more resistant to the integrating forces in American life. They preferred parish organization on ethnic lines and strove valiantly to preserve their language and customs. The Germans, who became the largest incoming group after the Civil War, believed that the loss of language was tantamount to the loss of faith.[15] Their emphasis on parochial schools, Catholic press, and social organizations had a strong cultural undertone.[16]

But the integrating forces in American culture and in Cathol-

14. Carl Wittke, *The Irish in America* (Baton Rouge: Louisiana State University Press, 1956), Chap. IX.
15. Colman J. Barry, *The Catholic Church and German Americans* (Milwaukee: Bruce Publishing Co., 1953).
16. The German Catholics sought greater representation on the hierarchy and supraparochial jurisdiction on national lines. The movement has been termed Cahenslyism after the founder of the immigrant aid society of St. Raphael.

icism proved irresistible. In the Church, as in the nation, the melting pot was effective.[17] The common sacramental and liturgical system aided, and even the official Latin was an asset. The fusing of the many cultural groups into a reasonably harmonious unity was achieved successfully, despite continued tension and occasional open conflict.

The integration of the immigrant into American life, described by Will Herberg as the major contribution of American Catholicism,[18] was only a by-product of the primary objective of the Church's leadership: to preserve his faith. Geographical mobility, especially from a rural to an urban environment, has always been a threat to religious practice. The same type of uprooted peasant who voyaged across the Atlantic was crowding into the industrial centers of Europe. Only a minority of these latter retained contact with a Catholicism that had been enmeshed in rural tradition but which could not adapt to the alien soil of industrial society.[19] The fact that in similar circumstances the majority did so in the United States has never been adequately explained. Unquestionably the favorable political atmosphere plus the social hostility were the important factors. A parallel might be found in those periods of Jewish history where there was no persecution to cripple his efforts yet enough discrimination to drive him into his group.

Viewed in this light, American Catholic history seems a unique achievement. But the grafting of the new elements on the original Anglo-American stock could not have taken place without extensive pruning. Sociologically, the Catholic immigrant had two divergent aims: he found it necessary to integrate himself into the general community; and he had to

17. The only notable schism was the minority Polish National Church.
18. *Protestant, Catholic, Jew* (New York: Doubleday, 1955). Henry Steele Commager, in *The American Mind* (New Haven: Yale University Press, 1950), p. 193, states: "It might indeed be maintained that the Catholic Church was, during the period [after 1880], one of the most effective of all agencies for democracy and Americanization."
19. See the author's, "The Dechristianization of the French Working Class," in *The Review of Politics*, Vol. 20, No. 1, pp. 46-69, Jan., 1958.

isolate himself from it to preserve his distinctive values, including his religious beliefs. Necessity pushed him into the mainstream of American life and opportunity beckoned in the marketplace. So powerful has been this thrust and so strong is the tendency of people in pluralistic societies to strive for the common denominator, that observers like Herberg believe that Catholics of a given class or region tend to respond very much like non-Catholics on questions such as sex, status seeking, economics, race, the role of government, and international relations. This view has received some confirmation in the few serious sociological studies that have been made in this field.[20] It has support in the urban concentration of American Catholics, as the dynamic of modern urban society is the desire to become acceptable to the dominant groups.

But if it were completely true there would be no reason for this book or for the tensions that demonstrably exist between Catholics and other Americans. Nor can the problem be exorcised by the thesis, so comforting to the anti-Catholic critic, that the American layman is enthralled by the hierarchy. Not only does the layman freely commit himself to the doctrine; but as he has risen educationally and become more articulate, he tends to rally behind his leadership on essential questions. The contemporary educated Catholic is certainly not the docile immigrant of yesteryear who depended upon the clergy to be his spokesman in all matters. He will be more critical of deficiencies in his leadership and less willing to be herded into the support of causes that are peripheral to his faith. But whereas the unusual individual who, in previous generations, rose from his immigrant group into academic distinction tended to lose his faith, today our secular university faculties have an increasing number of Catholic members, unquestionably loyal in doctrine and prac-

20. Joseph H. Fichter, *Southern Parish: The Dynamics of a City Parish* (Chicago: Chicago University Press, 1950); same, *Social Relations in a Northern Parish* (Chicago: Chicago University Press, 1954); and Joseph B. Schuyler, *Northern Parish: Sociological Analysis of an Urban Religious Social System* (Chicago: Loyola University Press, 1960).

**71**

tice. So it is in every field among men who are hardly blind followers of the hierarchy. What once may have been an immigrant identification has now become a conscious acceptance.

The American Catholic unquestionably shares many of the attitudes of his non-Catholic neighbors, especially those which relate to the means of achieving status in a bourgeois society. What differentiates him stems from his historical experience in America and the imperatives of his faith. The two are meshed, because his loyalty to the faith derives in part from the fact that Catholicism acted as a magnet to the lonely and disenchanted on arrival from abroad; that it offered them a buffer against social discrimination; and that it became their agency of assimilation into American life. But it was a loyalty which transcended the immigrant situation, as it has grown and deepened since large-scale European immigration ceased. It also provided the pattern for the assimilation of the more selective recent arrivals who came as refugees from totalitarianism. It is still unclear if it will be successful with the recent influx of Latin Americans, though there is reason to believe that it will.

The process of integrating the Catholic into American life did not proceed at an even pace. Almost imperceptible in the decades before the Civil War, it quickened as a consequence of the Catholic contribution to the great sectional conflict. By the end of the century there seemed a genuine opportunity for more complete acculturation. The Catholic body was beginning to be recognized on the national political scene and the rigid Protestant orthodoxy of earlier years tended to be replaced by more benevolent attitudes and by devotion to social service.

It was at this point that a vigorous group of clerical and lay leaders, of whom Archbishop John Ireland was the most dynamic spokesman, made a determined effort to achieve a more harmonious relation between Catholicism and American culture.[21] Success seemed assured despite the opposition of bishops like Corrigan, McQuaid, and a majority of the Germans who believed that Catholics must be insulated from an environment essentially harmful to their faith. The expectations of the "Americanizers" were disappointed less because of internal resistance than by the intrusion of European influences: French conservatives used the controversy to cast suspicion on the fidelity of American Catholics[22] and the Modernist issue paralyzed initiative in America and in the Church as a whole. Catholic scholarship as well as Catholic adjustment to a rapidly changing world were seriously damaged for several decades.

This in broad outline is the heritage of the American Catholic. What is of equal importance is the way in which he regards his past. When he does so he is not conscious of any serious gap between himself and the American tradition. This is reflected in his surprise when critics tell him that he does not belong. He feels at home in his culture and readily appropriates the leading personalities and events of American history as his own. Washington and Lincoln are his heroes, the American wars are his wars, the American expansion fills him with pride. This sets him apart from many European Catholics, particularly from the dominant mood in French Catholicism during the nineteenth century. To the majority of French Catholics of a generation ago and earlier, the Revolution of 1789 was a great watershed that separated them from the happier time when the Church presided in a privileged position over the destiny of the nation. It was this concern with a situation which time had made obsolete which produced the French Catholic Right, just as a growing awareness of the folly

21. Robert D. Cross, *The Emergence of Liberal Catholicism in America* (Cambridge: Harvard University Press, 1958); John Tracy Ellis, *The Life of James Cardinal Gibbons,* two vols. (Milwaukee: Bruce Publishing Co., 1952); J. H. Moynihan, *The Life of Archbishop John Ireland* (New York: Harper & Bros., 1953).
22. Thomas T. McAvoy, *The Great Crisis in American Catholic History, 1895-1900* (Chicago: Henry Regnery Co., 1957); Abbé Félix Klein, *Une Hérésie fantôme,* Vol. VI of *Souvenirs* (Paris: Plon, 1948).

of this backward glance created the French Catholic **Left.**

The American Catholic has never been so obsessed with a sense of the tragedy of his history. In the literal meaning of the term there is no American Catholic reactionary for there is no conceivable American past to which he might wish to return. Certain individuals have romanticized about the Middle Ages, but this was an aesthetic cult or a polemical response to an overcritical historical interpretation of the "Age of Faith." At any event it is dead today. The eclipse of the Gothic in contemporary church building is more than a change in style.

American Catholics do not divide into "Left" and "Right" as passionately as did their European brethren—certainly not for the same reasons. Conservative and liberal trends surely exist. But their roots tend to lie, in the American Catholic past as well as present, in divergent attitudes toward American culture and the possibility open to American Catholicism to play a constructive role within its framework. This is the central issue. The pessimist will admit that Catholicism has been able to grow within the context of a Protestant environment. He will concede that the erosion of Protestant aggressiveness has contributed to the advance. But he remains basically insecure even when he admits that the presidential election of 1960 marked a decisive point in the acceptance of the Catholic in the national life.

Were one to probe for the root of this insecurity at a time when he should be developing confidence and a sense of responsibility, one would find that this pessimist is disturbed by his reading of contemporary trends in American life. The American culture he wishes to identify with is not the one which he sees undergoing rapid change but the one he regards as threatened by these changes. He is very happy with the residuum of Protestantism which still informs our legal and political institutions, and which has been operative in our moral life and in our public education—"Protestantism without its bite," as it may be described. If he be historically minded he will know that it was not Catholicism which fed these waters of spiritual vitality into the American stream. But whether he is historically informed or not, this was the America he loved and which he desperately wishes to maintain. What he is particularly anxious to preserve is the atmosphere of religion which Protestantism injected into American public life, not as it was at its point of origin but as remembered in the recent past. That this feeling goes beyond the pessimists may be symbolized by the growing tendency of Catholics to celebrate Thanksgiving religiously. Gone are the days, described by Peter Finlay Dunne, when we celebrated Thanksgiving to thank God for being delivered from the Pilgrims, as they once did for being delivered from the Indians. The growing number of American Catholics who go with their families to their parish churches on Thanksgiving morning are certainly thanking God for being Americans. They may be hoping that something of the Pilgrim tradition may be salvaged.

For those who may be termed pessimists in these matters, this represents a considerable change of focus. In Ireland's time, the conservative opposition decried the Archbishop's experiment in Faribault, Minnesota, where a parochial school was subsidized by the local school board, on the grounds that no provision had been made to limit its pupils to Catholic children. Nor was this an isolated instance. As present-day opponents of public school prayer and Bible reading delight to remind us, it was often Catholic protests and Catholic fears of Protestant influence that acted as a solvent of the religious orientation of our public schools.

What has changed is the nature of the fears. No longer is it, at least in most sections of the country, the proselytizing of the Protestant that is considered a threat, but now it is the determined antireligious position of the secularist. The insecure Catholic of a half century ago would have fixed on the dominant Protestant temper of the public school as the danger to the faith of the Catholic student; those of similar mentality today would view the vestigial religious observances in public schools as desirable links between religion and the nation.

Fears about the direction American culture is taking would

be one ingredient in a conservative Catholic position. But this could be shared by many to whom it would remain as a fact of sociological analysis. It becomes a source of action when it is given an emotional thrust and when it is reinforced by other factors. One such would be the conviction that hard-won social status or financial position was being undermined by governmental policy. This social conservatism has received scant support from official Catholic doctrine which has strongly inclined toward a welfare concept of the state. But the very intensity of the drive of the immigrant and of his descendants to make his way under the American rules— traditionally laissez-faire—may cause consternation when the rules are changed. It is as though a family labored hard to achieve the status of a Cadillac only to find the Volkswagon fashionable. Welfare and social security policies, unknown in the rugged days when many immigrants were on the slope, may seem wasteful now that the heights are in prospect.

Perhaps the most potent cause of American Catholic conservatism is a reflex of the appreciation he feels for the country with which he has identified himself. If there is any sociological reality in America today, it is the deep patriotism of the average Catholic. It is very obvious that the practice of Catholicism is considered a favorable factor in assaying the reliability of a person for a security post. Internationally minded Catholics complain of the narrowness of this nationalist feeling, but they share it in some degree. Catholics with a professional interest in ethics deplored the silence of American Catholics when obliteration bombing and ultimately nuclear weapons were employed by their country in World War II, but these critics have found their own voice since the war was won. A sincere patriotism is the index of the gratitude of the American Catholic for what his country has offered him, and it is as wide as the Catholic community. "For God and Country" is not merely chiseled on the stones of Catholic institutions; it is found in the hearts of those who pass through them.

Perhaps the historian's dictum that nationalism begins as a revolutionary force and ends as a conservative phenomenon may apply here. Certainly it explains the depth of the American Catholic's reaction to communism which surprises European Catholics. To the former the threat is two-dimensional: one prong is aimed at the country he loves, the other at his religion. Abstractly this is true of every American of every religious persuasion. If there is a difference in the vigor of the Catholic's response, it must be explained by the closeness of the identification he has made with his country and by the fact that he is made aware of the realities by verifiable stories of atrocities to fellow Catholics in Eastern Europe and in mission lands. These create a trauma in the American Catholic comparable to the Jewish reaction to Naziism. When religious persecution is added to the anti-American propaganda of the Cold War the pressure becomes explosive.

Every believing American Catholic is resolutely anti-Communist. What differs is the emotional index in the response. The majority are partially immunized by the traditional American faith that all will work out well. But when opposition to communism is reinforced by a pessimistic interpretation of the state of American culture and when it is buttressed by conservative social views, the combination can become dangerous to the person concerned and to the nation which he aims to defend. Only a tiny minority of American Catholics have joined with an equally small minority of non-Catholics in extremist organizations. But while their stridency attracts attention, it should not distract us from the complex roots of their psychosis.

Those Americans who may be alarmed to find Catholics in extremist patriotic groups may take comfort in a much deeper tendency in contemporary American Catholicism: the growth of self-criticism. The significance of this is as profound as its manifestation is unmistakable. If there is any sign in an individual or a group which reveals self-assurance, it is the open analysis of his own faults. It never occurs when one considers oneself as camping in the midst of the enemy. When one assays his situation as a state of siege, self-imposed security regulations are severe. One does not reveal one's pimples lest they be exposed as warts. Any deeper diagnosis of one's failures is avoided lest it give comfort to those outside the walls. The tragedy of this is, as Santayana remarked, that when an individual or a group does not honestly examine its mistakes, it is doomed to repeat them.

Self-criticism was impossible for the American Catholic as long as *Maria Monk* was the standard by which his efforts were judged. Even today a Catholic in official position is assured that each month his mail will contain a tract which "proves", through carefully selected quotations from Catholic sources, that he belongs to a group with the most nefarious purposes. Not so long ago Paul Blanshard carried this technique to a new level of sophistication by the addition of footnotes. It would still be an instructive exercise to collect the reviews of his books from popular and even reputedly serious journals.

It is not that this curious polemic of proving Catholics sinners from their own words has died in the United States. What has changed is the attitude of Catholics. Till approximately the Second World War tendentious attacks were taken seriously and resented as the older immigrant used to reject bad jokes about his nationality. The result was that Catholics were generally careful to present everything in the most favorable light. Scholarly works of history or philosophy might warily touch upon the blemishes in the record. But there was danger even here, for the Blanshard-type searchlight probed into the inner recesses of the professional library.

Dramatically, devastatingly, this has changed. There is a temptation to fix the point of departure at Monsignor Ellis's critical assessment of Catholic higher education.[23] Certainly an analysis of the shortcomings of Catholic colleges and universities would touch sensitive spots. They had been built at

23. Published in *Thought* as "American Catholics and the Intellectual Elite," No. 30 (Autumn, 1955), pp. 351-388.

immense sacrifice; they had demonstrably improved since their shaky begininings; and they were under increasing competition from public institutions with unlimited funds. To expose their deficiencies could be interpreted in Catholic circles as the great betrayal. This is the way it seemed to a few who criticized the Ellis article. But the unexpected happened as well: the learned historian from Catholic University was supported in public print by the ex-president of Notre Dame, Father John Cavanaugh, and by practically the entire Catholic academic community. Though the press and news weeklies had a happy time recording comments on the absence of Catholic Einsteins, Catholic college faculties and organizations like the National Catholic Educational Association got down to the hard work of appraisal and improvement.

Perhaps this was the spring thaw. Soon the dam burst and every aspect of American Catholic life was inundated by a flood of critical comment from Catholics. This did not remain on the high level of the scholarly quarterly. It reached down to the house organs aimed at the average Catholic. A particularly noteworthy role was played by the Jesuit weekly *America,* and its editors were surprised by the astounding jump in circulation which coincided with the new approach. To illustrate: the issue of October 20, 1962 carried an article, *The Council Opens,* which explored the meaning of Pope John's frequently used word *aggiornmento*—a bringing up to date of Catholic thought and practice. While this may be passed over as a simple recognition of the need of improvement in the Church, the following issue's *The Council: A Lesson from the Past,* used the experience of Cardinal Newman in dealing with the Roman congregations to make observations that are flattering to the former but hardly to the latter. As a partial conclusion, it states:

It remains, then, for the Second Vatican Council to translate into effective action the widespread conviction that if the faithful are expected to obey their ecclesiastical superiors exercising juridical power, so also the hierarchy must become responsive to the Spirit in the faithful when the latter exercise their charismatic authority, and authority of conscience and truth.

It is beyond question that the problem of freedom and authority in the Church would be less acute today if the lessons of the 19th century had been assimilated. One lesson is this: the greater the concentration of authority, the greater the temptation not only to disregard the opinions of others but even to suppress them. In the 19th century, there arose within the Church—and it could happen again— a party which elevated its own opinions into dogmas and sought to expose all schools of thought but its own. Such a party, Newman perceived, works havoc wih consciences, destroys union in charity, and throws up a roadblock in the path of inquirers.[24]

It is writing such as this which explains the favorable reception in Catholic journals and in the Catholic reading public of Hans Küng's adventurous, *The Council, Reform, and Reunion.*[25] A number of American bishops used this book to prepare themselves for their work at the Council. One would have to read this German Catholic theologian's interpretation of the Protestant Reformation and the current need for reform in the Church to appreciate how mature American Catholics had become to accept such drastic revisions of popularly held assumptions. Yet for one Catholic journal which entered a *caveat,* there were dozens which cheered.

This new realism in American Catholic attitudes has led to a rather modest reassessment of their role in the national history as the Church nears the completion of the second century of its organized existence in our midst. Eliminating necessary explanations and with the risk of oversimplification, the current estimate would go something like this: until the present generation, there was little realization among American Catholics that they had responsibility for society as a whole. Till

24. Vincent F. Blehl, Oct. 27, 1962, p. 950.
25. New York: Sheed & Ward, 1961.

**80**

then, their posture had been mainly defensive. Their preoccupation has been with the defense of the faith. It has been this consideration that supplied the dynamic for their greatest achievement: the establishment of their educational system. When they entered into the public forum, it was largely to perform rear-guard actions in favor of legislation regarding morality, particularly on those issues which concerned marriage and the family. They did smile benignly on the labor movement and in the Bishops' Statement on Social Reconstruction (1919), they produced a positive document of prime importance which foreshadowed many of the reforms of the New Deal.[26] In this fight for social justice the principal contribution of the bishops was their insistence that society is a moral organism in wihch there must be a mutual sharing of advantages and burdens. Slow to enter the field of Negro rights because so few of their own were involved, American Catholics have recently done a good deal through the Bishops' Letter of 1958,[27] through the Catholic Interracial Councils, and through the insistence of some bishops on the moral evil of segregation with consequent action in Catholic schools and institutions. The Catholic community has made notable contributions to public welfare and has been particularly blessed by a long series of outstanding women who have founded religious communities for social work, women such as Mother Elizabeth Seton, Mother Katherine Drexel, and Mother Rose Hawthorne.[28] Only recently have they become aware of their international responsibilities, although again in the charitable field of overseas relief and refugee resettlement their record

26. Raphael M. Huber, ed., *Our Bishops Speak* (Milwaukee: Bruce Publishing Co., 1952), pp. 46-51. For background see Patrick W. Gearty, *The Economic Thought of Monsignor John A. Ryan* (Washington: Catholic University Press, 1953); Mary Harrita Fox, *Peter E. Dietz, Labor Priest* (Notre Dame: Notre Dame University Press, 1953).
27. This magnificent report "On Compulsory Segregation" was made by the American hierarchy at its annual meeting Nov. 13, 1958. *Catholic Mind*, Vol. LVII, No. 114, Jan.-Feb., 1959.
28. A romantic example is found in the Journal of one of the pioneers in the West, Sister Blandina Segale, *At the End of the Sante Fe Trail* (Milwaukee: Bruce Publishing Co., 1948).

is superb. Even more recently Catholics have awakened to the challenge of urbanization and housing which vitally affects so many of their fellow Catholics.

This is not offered as a litany and it has deliberately ignored what all Catholics would agree is their primary purpose: to lead men to God through Christ. What has been attempted is to show that circumstances and internal preoccupations have circumscribed the public effort of Catholics in the past, but that they now have reached the stage in their development in which it is possible for them to make a massive contribution to American life. Whether they do so or not will depend on how they react to the new world that is constantly emerging. In political parlance: history has taken them to a New Frontier where they will be tested by different standards.

Before attempting to estimate the nature of the issues which confront him, we must look at the American Catholic in a wider context. For although he has been deeply influenced by his experience in this country, he is the heir of a long history and of a body of belief that was articulated before he came to the New World. The Catholic is, like other Americans, a projection from Europe where his basic heritage was forged. As a product of the Atlantic community, he has continued to be shaped by events across the ocean. His center of religious authority is there, and from the older areas of Catholicism he has drawn his inspiration. From Europe came nearly all of his membership, the bulk of his clergy in the formative period, the funds that permitted him to survive, and the moral courage that helped him endure.

Even today when his dependence on Europe for men and material aid has practically disappeared, the American Catholic is still indebted to the older lands abroad. Nearly all the movements which hold contemporary promise in the American Church had their origin and development in Europe: the surge in Biblical study and research; the participation of the laity in the liturgy and in the work of the Church; the acceptance of art forms more suited to the modern temperament; the opening of new horizons in historiography, in religious sociology, and in philosophical thought. It has been the Catholic intellectual who has been the immediate beneficiary of this wealth of new material that has been made available to him. It is this that has sustained him in his hopeful attitude toward the possibilities of his Church in the modern world. But through him the inspiration is gradually filtering down, receiving in the process its characteristic American adaptation.

But if he has inherited the strengths of European Catholicism, he has been spared some, though not all, of its burdens. To appreciate his link with the more remote religious past, we need to recall that the three historic religions of our civilization have a common root in the Old Testament. Biblical religion was distinguished from others by its strong ethical flavor. It was not content with a profession of God's existence. Its aims were to influence man's conduct and to lead him to God. The Hebrew prophet not only spoke in the name of God; he passed judgment in God's name on human action. To the man of the Old Testament, everything which man did had its dignity only in relation to God. No part of human life lay outside the divine scrutiny. Man was urged to turn to God at every stage of life, at every part of his day, and in all his needs. The aim of Biblical religion was to consecrate—to make holy or God-centered—all of man's mundane activity.

The three great religions of the West were historic in a twofold sense: their validity depended on concrete events that were subject to rational inquiry; and to effect their purpose they had to enter into the stream of history and become identified with man's interests. To the degree in which they became incarnate in given historical situations they were able to achieve their end. Thus Judaism demonstrated its adaptability to the conditions of the Diaspora, Christianity in finding its place in the Graeco-Roman world, and Islam in its passage from the desert to the sophisticated surroundings of Bagdad or Cordova.

But the demand for this adjustment was continuous, since change is the essence of history. There is always the danger that the very success which an historic religion has in reaching man at a particular stage of his cultural development, might imperil its capacity to move to a new. Thus Western Christianity showed itself remarkably resilient in meeting the sweeping changes of the long period we call Medieval. But its very fruitful interaction with the culture of the thirteenth century contributed to its difficulty in responding to the new forces which had appeared by the end of the fifteenth. The index of the failure was the Protestant Reformation and the fragmentation of Christianity.

Not only did this weaken Christianity's influence, but it aided kings and princes in their effort to gan practical control over whatever church existed in their territory and to compel the highest degree of compliance with it on the part of their subjects. Thus there appeared the new phenomenon of the national church where the state exercised its influence over the church it declared "established" as it offered it protection and support.

From this situation there emerged three issues in the post-Reformation period. One was an older question: shall the man of religion regard the world as hopeless and abandon it to its own devices by retreating into his inner conscience where alone he can find security? While such a view might find support in many of Luther's statements, no Christian religious group adopted it as a permanent policy.

The second was the attitude of religious groups toward functions which churches had once performed and which they were now progressively losing to public agencies. There had been a period in Europe's past when the bankruptcy of the central political authority encouraged men to look to the Church to perform essential services. Often this went to the point of the creation of ecclesiastical states where clerics wielded direct political power. Ordinarily they provided many of the public services on which the community depended.

The Reformation had swept away most of the former and had encouraged the growing monarchical states to whittle away at the latter. But there were still many contradictions in this field in seventeenth and eighteenth century Europe. There were still the Papal States and the prince Bishoprics of the Rhineland; the churches still performed essential roles in keeping vital statistics, in regulating marriage and wills, and in welfare and education. It was the French Revolution and its accompanying movements, along with the whole fabric of events in the nineteenth century, which finally stripped the churches of the public aspect of these activities, though generally they were allowed to perform some of them on a voluntary basis.

This whole process is termed the secularization of Western culture. But as often happens with words we use for such broad movements, the term is ambiguous. In the exact sense secularization was the reabsorption by lay authorities of responsibilities which clerics had assumed when the civil power was too weak to fulfill them. Here secularization was a normal concomitant of the growth of government. It was healthy in the sense that there is no special reason why a bishop should be in charge of roads or defense. That he might have been resulted from historical accidents and was in no way connected with his spiritual mission. However, when a situation becomes institutionalized, change may be difficult. If too abrupt, conflict may result. It might be said of this aspect of secularization what David Thomson wrote of the French Law of Separation of 1905: "Carried through in different circumstances, the Separation would have had a healing effect like a skillful surgery. . . . But . . . Church and State were torn apart, not neatly separated; and political bitterness was fed with new fuel."[29]

But secularization has a second meaning: the elimination of religion from all public life by confining it to the private de-

29. *Democracy in France: The Third Republic* (New York: Oxford University Press, 1946), p. 143.

votion of the individual. This is what some European secularists meant by "driving religion into the sacristy." French historians make the distinction between *laïcité*, the transfer of public functions from clerical to lay control, and *laïcisme*, an aggressive assault on the role of religion in society. The consequences of the second were more serious. Historically the concept of limited government, which is at the root of democracy, grew out of government's recognition of the Church as independent of its control. The elimination of organized religion as a check to state power gives a degree of plausibility to Professor Jacob Talmon's thesis that Radical Jacobinism was the father of modern totalitarianism.[30]

What made it more difficult for men to distinguish between a legitimate secularism that was inherent in the whole course of modern European history and the secularism that was antagonistic to any independent role for religion was that the two were often combined in the same persons and movements. The avowed determination of the antireligious minorities of the eighteenth and nineteenth century often made defenders of the *status quo* resistant to necessary adjustment.

The third issue was what to do with the minorities which dissented from the dominant creed in the states of post-Reformation Europe. In an earlier age when the only minority ordinarily had been the Jews, the problem, unhappily, had never been justly resolved. Now in many states predominantly Catholic there were Protestant groups; in Protestant states there were Catholic and dissenting Protestant minorities. As time passed there were individuals everywhere who rejected all religion.

The solution of this problem was retarded by the bitterness arising out of the religious struggle of the Reformation. But it was complicated by a deeper question: what is needed for men to live in social harmony in a political community? It has always been obvious that the pull of self-interest threatens

30. J. L. Talmon, *Political Messianism* (New York: Frederick A. Praeger, 1960).

any social unit and certainly any state. From the time of the Stoics it was recognized that these centrifugal tendencies must be balanced in a political community by a common will to live together which can be expressed in some common assumptions or fixed points of reference to which all can adhere. This came to be known as the *consensus*, an agreed ground for community action.

Traditionally in Western history this political consensus had been a religious bond. Since it had been the only one known, it was assumed that it would be the only one which would work. This explains why early modern kings with little personal interest in religion were so insistent on religious conformity within their boundaries. To them it was a political necessity. Certainly the men who wrote the Civil Constitution of the Clergy during the French Revolution (1790) could hardly be accused of burning religious zeal. Yet in their own words religion was to be the tie which bound men to the state so that it could demand obedience as a sacred duty. Here they were not far from Rousseau who had proposed a civic religion to which men would be forced to subscribe. The Civil Constitution was not an expression of the separation of church and state in the modern sense. It was intended as a recognition of the importance of a state-controlled religion in maintaining national unity. Old ways die hard.

But die they did. The first note in the requiem was sounded in the new Republic born of the American Revolution. There is no doubt that the ideas of the Enlightenment had some influence in preparing the American leadership for the revolt, though these ideas took on a different coloration when they crossed the Atlantic. But the decisive factor was pragmatic: in no other way could the thirteen states, four of which had established churches and all of which had a mosaic of religious variations, be formed into a single nation.[31] Thus was born

31. Clinton Rossiter, *Seedtime of the Republic* (New York: Harcourt, Brace, 1953), is essential for the intellectual background of the Constitutional period.

the pluralist society. It did not claim that no consensus was necessary. On the contrary it professed a set of ultimates and even would demand assent to these when crises would arise.[32] But it allowed each citizen to explain these basic propositions in any religious or philosophical manner he chose. Man was to be free in matters religious—to be a Catholic, Protestant, Jew, or freethinker. No previous Act of Toleration had included all of these. Here was a new concept, and it had appeared more as a result of expediency than conviction.

What had been hammered out through stern necessity at the time of our national origin was to occur in all modern states in the years that followed. What was decisive was the manner of its coming. In only one European country was its appearance as smooth as in the United States. In Belgium the Catholic majority found the means of coexistence with a liberal ex-Catholic minority to achieve national independence in 1830. The two groups then wrote full religious liberty into the Constitution.[33]

The reaction of Catholics to the growth of pluralism in other countries was in large part determined by the concrete historical situation. In some, such as England, Canada, Australia, New Zealand, Switzerland, the Netherlands, Scandinavia and much of Eastern Europe, Catholics lived in a society largely non-Catholic. Here they were the beneficiaries and supporters of any move toward toleration. In a few, Ireland and Poland, they lived in a society overwhelmingly Catholic but controlled by a foreign and non-Catholic power. Here the issues of religious and political liberty were merged and both were strengthened in the process. In some, France, Italy, and Austria, Catholics fought stubbornly against the disintegration of the religious consensus, but ultimately learned to live with

32. The Smith Act is a classic instance. Others could be cited to indicate that our society is willing to grant freedom to the point where it considers itself imperiled.
33. It is regrettable that the Belgian experience is not better known in this country. Its origin is set forth in Henri Haag, *Les Origines du Catholicsme libéral en Belgique, 1789-1839* (Louvain, 1950).

it. In a few, Spain and some Latin American countries, Catholics have refused to concede the fact of pluralism and still see religious unity as essential for national cohesion.

What stands out in the record is that the appearance of pluralism in modern history was not willed but was a product of circumstances. It did not appear as much from a set of ideas as from facts. Since practical necessity was its dynamic, it was not rigidly ideological, but capable of development.

The second conclusion is obvious: American Catholics were the pioneers in adjusting to a pluralist society. Just as they showed the possibility and advantages of living under a republican and democratic form of government, so they were to demonstrate to their European confreres, the merits of pluralism. In this way they have repaid, rather amply, their debt to the more ancient Catholicism across the seas.

A European might incline to minimize the achievement of the American Catholic on the ground that it was made in a favorable climate where religion was officially respected and where it was reflected to some degree in the activities of the community. Certainly this has been true. American pluralism was not conceived, as so often in Europe, in any spirit of hostility to religion. Many prominent leaders in our formative period were not active communicants;[34] some were not professedly Christian. Jefferson was typical of the latter. While suspicious of the motives of ministers, he did indicate his belief in the practical role of religion. When he made his proposals for the projected University of Virginia he suggested that the various creeds should establish religious centers adjacent to the campus so that the students could receive the moral benefits of religious training.

It is abundantly clear that the pioneers of modern pluralism

---

34. This was true in later periods as the case of Lincoln testifies. No man more deeply grounded his life and his action on religion, but he was not a churchgoer. His proclamation of May 30, 1863, should be read by every American.

welcomed the impulses deriving from religion. Rossiter summarizes the evidence:

> The men of 1776 believed that the good state would rise on the rock of private and public morality, that morality was, in the case of most men and all states, the product of religion, and that the earthly mission of religion was to set men free. It was no mere pose when they justified resistance to oppression as obedience to God and an appeal to heaven.[35]

It was in this spirit that a select group approached the problem of writing an organic law for the new nation. As men of their age, they were steeped in the spirit of the Natural Law which they derived from their English origins.[36] It was on this ground of Natural Law and Natural Rights that they would establish a rule of law in which the government's sovereignty would be limited by the God-given rights of the individual and by the required consent of the people. Because they held that man had rights prior to his status as a citizen, they made the distinction between society and government which is a precondition for any defense of freedom.[37]

In the body of the Constitution which resulted from their efforts, there was only one reference to religion. In Article VI it was stated that there should be no religious test for office. The words "state," "church," and "separation" do not appear in any form in the text. It was the First Congress which made essential additions with the ten amendments, placing as the First: "Congress shall make no law respecting the estab-

35. *Ibid.*, p. 59.
36. Jacques Maritain, *Man and the State* (Chicago: Chicago University Press, 1951), pp. 95ff.; John Courtney Murray, *We Hold These Truths* (New York: Sheed & Ward, 1960), lists the three fundamentals of Natural Law as: acceptance of man as intelligent; of reality as intelligible; and the conviction that once reality is grasped by intelligence, it poses an obligation to obey prior to human legislation. Yet there is no doubt that Catholic support of Natural Law today is the great dividing line between the Catholic and non-Catholic concept of morality.
37. Robert M. MacIver, *The Web of Government* (New York: Macmillan, 1947), pp. 31-32.

lishment of religion, or prohibiting the free exercise thereof. . . ."

There is no doubt that the purpose of this amendment, as of the others, was to buttress the defense of the individual against the state and in a most important area. This was a limitation placed upon government in dealing with its citizens. It appears from the text, reinforced by the general thinking of the period, that the prohibition against establishment was affirmed in order to protect religious freedom. Religious liberty was the objective, no establishment the means. That the First Congress was not motivated by hostility toward religion is clear from its action in providing chaplains for both houses of Congress and for the armed services at government expense. It also reenacted the North-West Ordinance (1790), originally passed in 1787, which stated:

> Religion, morality, and knowledge, being necessary for good citizenship and the happiness of mankind, schools and the means of education shall forever be encouraged.

In American practice the Constitution includes not only the text but the relevant decisions of the Supreme Court. For more than a century and a half the Court interpreted this charter of religious freedom in its obvious sense: government could not give a privileged position to any church but could promote the religious interests of all citizens. This is how it ruled in 1892 in the *Church of the Holy Trinity* vs. *the United States:*

> The Constitution of every one of the 44 states contains language which either directly or by clear implication recognizes a profound reverence for religion and an assumption that its influence is essential for the well-being of the community. . . .

> There is no dissonance in these declarations. There is a universal language pervading them all having one meaning:

they affirm and reaffirm that this is a religious nation. These are not individual sayings, declarations of private persons; they are organic utterances; they speak the voice of the entire people . . . Because of the general recognition of this truth the question has seldom been presented to the courts.[38]

The same spirit informed Justice William Douglas's majority opinion in upholding released time in the Zorach case (1952):

We are a religious people whose institutions presuppose the existence of a Supreme Being. . . . When the state encourages religious instruction . . . it follows the best of our traditions. For it then respects the religious nature of our people and accommodates the public service to their spiritual needs. . . . We cannot read into the Bill of Rights a philosophy of hostility to religion.[39]

Beyond both the text and the decisions, the Constitution rests on the tradition and attitudes of the people, for in the American system government is an agent which must be responsive to the public will. Popular interest in religion in the United States was greatly stimulated during the first quarter of the nineteenth century by the Great Awakening. This wave of enthusiasm for Evangelical Protestantism might have proved a threat to religious pluralism, but the structure was rooted enough to remain. As the century progressed the intensity of religious concern lessened, though there is adequate evidence that still "we are a religious people."

In our entire constitutional history the emphasis has been on the citizen. Because the citizen was the focus of government, there was no difficulty, constitutional or otherwise, when Congress passed the G.I. Bill allowing veterans to use government funds for education in the school of their choice. Because the stress here had been placed on the citizen who

38.  143 U.S. 457 (1892).
39.  343 U.S. 314 (1952).

JOSEPH N. MOODY

had served his country, there was no objection when some used these funds to study for the ministry or rabbinate in a seminary. This principle of the primacy of the citizen extends to all fields for it is the citizen who exercises the various rights guaranteed by the Constitution, who determines public policy by his vote at the polls and his voice in the public forum, and who makes the other choices which he believes will enrich his life. The government remains neutral, not entering into the choice of its citizens nor influencing their decisions. Impartiality is its keynote as its citzens freely select the means they will employ to satisfy their needs.

How this satisfaction is obtained is an important part of the pluralist society. "Pluralist" refers to many groups and, as the British seem to realize more clearly than ourselves, the success of this type of free society depends in great part on its capacity to encourage citizens to perform voluntary services which will contribute to the common good. It is the vitality of these groups which ensures the public good. We can glimpse their importance when we note the practice of all totalitarian states. Not only do they repress religious freedom and free opinion but they control human activity by replacing pluralist by monopolistic social controls. The complex social organization of the free society disappears and its place is taken by manipulated social organizations.[40]

Professor Robert MacIver's analysis of the multigroup society shows that the balance and interadjustment of many elements are more desirable than the all-inclusive, all-regulating state. "The wells of knowledge and inspiration are not less full for the number who drink of them." This, he shows, is particularly true of man's cultural interests which are exceedingly diverse. It is in this field that the attitudes of the various segments vary most profoundly: "To coordinate them all into one mould would be to destroy their characteristic qualities,

40. For the Nazi methods see Franz Neumann, *Behemoth: The Structure and Practice of National Socialism* (New York: Oxford University Press, 1944), pp. 400ff.

93

to drain them of their vitality." The state cannot be all-embracing for every way of life and every way of thought is nourished from within.[41]

It is hoped that the relevance of these observations will appear when we discuss the role of government in education. Actually few question the value to society of voluntary activities, as when one group devotes its energies to the humanitarian enterprises of the Red Cross, another to the support of Harvard College, a third to the preservation of historic sites, and a fourth to the welfare of youth in YMCA or YMHA. In effect the government recognizes the social utility of many of these activities by granting them tax favors.

A pluralist society is open, not only because it encourages the spontaneous grouping of its citizens, but because its non-ideological character assures continual development. While its original formulators laid down certain fixed points that should guide its development—this is the meaning of the amendments—it would be unrealistic to suppose that the needs of contemporary society could be met in the same way as that of our Fathers. It is precisely this flexibility to change that produces disagreement and conflict. Today there are three areas in which Catholics often find themselves in opposition to other Americans. These, which will occupy our attention for the remainder of this paper, are: the recognition of religion in public life; the relation of legislation to morality; and the role of religion in education.

Perhaps none of these can be solved on the level of abstract principles. But the viability of American democracy has been its capacity to adjust to practical needs and to find temporary solutions for complex problems. A case in point is the American public school system which was not originally proposed as an ideal but as a working compromise that all could live with. Further, European political scientists delight in reminding us that on the basis of abstract considerations our constitu-

41. *The Web of Government* (New York: Macmillan, 1947), pp. 421ff.

tional system should not work at all. That it does, with relative efficiency, they ascribe to the good sense of those who operate it since these refuse to push to the ultimate the latent conflicts embodied in our constitutional text.

Before discussing the position of religion in public life, a brief survey of the nature of politics is necessary. When Aristotle defined man as a political animal he meant that man was a community-building animal by his very nature. No one can build anything without intruding his purposes into the construction. When one builds a community, he must make choices, and choices will depend on what one seeks, on one's values. Thus morality which involves the free human being in his role of making choices is inherent in the political process.

But the making of community decisions, which is the core of politics, is too complex to be reduced to the moral factor. Man does not merely conceive an ideal society and then devise means to achieve it, or as much of it as possible. But while factors other than the moral enter, the moral cannot be excluded, for if it were, the decision would be nothing more than the will of the strongest. It is obvious that without an appeal to morality the plight of the Negro in American society would be hopeless.

Yet the same case of the Negro shows that in addition to morality, or justice in the classic authors, politics includes the right of the state to command, in the last resort, the material resources of the whole community and the total obedience of its members. While any state, and notably one like ours which is based on a theory of limited government, will use compulsion as sparingly as possible, the threat of force lies always in the shadows. The need to employ it diminishes in proportion as the interests of the citizen coincide with those of the state, and to the degree in which the citizen builds a habit of loyalty and an attitude of affection toward his community.

A third element in the process is the making and registering of compromises. Government is constructive when it helps groups to reconcile differences and to strike bargains which government will then safeguard through legislation. Thus the state provides the framework by which bodies of men with different convictions are encouraged to live in mutual peace and helpfulness.

Thus it would be naïve to regard morality and justice as the sole factor in determining community action. But it is an essential ingredient which must concern the whole community. Religious groups, of course, will be primarily concerned with it. Every religion conceives its essential purpose as the deepening in man of an awareness of God. But all our historic religions realize that this cannot be achieved by directing man's attention exclusively to the Supreme Being. Man's regard and his love must also extend outward to all creatures and to all human beings. To the question in the early pages of Genesis, "Am I my brother's keeper?" every religion derived from the Bible gives an unqualified affirmative. "As a living faith must change the life of a believer, so a living religion must influence and transform the social way of life. . . ."[42]

But religion should not be alone in its interest in morality. The community, too, must define its goals, its values, and the standards by which it will reach them. The president of Notre Dame University in an address to the National Science Foundation argued that science has the power to become the greatest liberator of mankind but "is prostituted to something far below its greatest human potentiality." What is needed is a review of values:

> To the hungry of the world we give the image of stored surpluses, better dog food, more esoteric dishes, how to eat more and still lose weight, how to have more appetite and then alleviate the effects of overeating, how to stimulate and then sedate.
>
> Better soap, better deodorants, better cars, better cigarettes, better heating and cooling, better barbiturates, better

42. Christopher Dawson, *The Historic Reality of Christian Culture* (New York: Harper & Bros., 1960), p. 68.

chewing gum: These seem to be the ultimate blessings that science and technology have afforded us.[43]

What is of the greatest concern, he concluded, was the fate of the rest of humanity; but we will have to decide that this is the task of the highest priority.

There is an element of conscious exaggeration here. The operative phrase is "to decide." Apart from the need each of us has to know his own objectives, there is a special urgency today for Americans to clarify their values. Our position of world leadership is a reality, and no group can exercise leadership unless it can define what it wants to happen: what sort of peace, justice, and sanity it proposes to work for in a disjointed world. Anti-communism as a base for action is demonstrably unworkable, for no achievement can be built upon negatives. History demands that we should be able to declare not only what we stand for, but why.

Should religion play any role in shaping the values of the American people? Certainly this has been its historic role. To fulfill its function, any church must be the conscience of its community. This is a delicate task which does not win many accolades while it is being performed. Curiously, it is the basis of man's ultimate judgment upon it. We are inclined to praise a man for all seasons like Thomas More who was "the King's good servant but God's first"; or the bishop who preached on kingly responsibility before Louis XIV; or the church leader who defied the Nazis. Silence on any of these occasions is judged harshly by posterity and the religious sycophant rarely wins enduring praise. Even the nonbeliever lauds the martyr—after he has died. But often as not it was popular fury, roused by the martyr's rejection of what was considered immediately desirable, that brought about his death. The Hebrew prophet remains the prototype of much that is admired in religion; but there is little evidence that the people of his time hailed him for his positive thinking. Here is a

43. Rev. Theodore Hesburgh, *New York Times*, Nov. 17, 1962, p. 28.

dilemma which every religious leader faces: he may be called upon to oppose the wishes of his people without absolute assurance that his position will be proved correct with time.

If the man of religion is to exercise the prophetic function, as needs he must, it is important that he undertake it with the accents of persuasion and with the hope of lifting man's vision and of inculcating the twofold principle of love as it applies to the social process. It is even more important—critics will say it is rare—that the religious spokesman approach his task humbly realizing that while his divine message may bear truth, he who proclaims it is a sinful human. Whether he be Jew or Christian, he will not find warrant in his faith that all human ills can be cured or that a perfect world can be formed. Both religion and experience indicate that man's possibilities for improvement will remain limited for the very reason that he will forever remain self-centered.

It is the purpose of religion to reduce human self-centeredness by directing man's energies toward God and his fellow men. The British historian Butterfield has defined civilization as mutual arrangements in restraint of self-interest. He points out that when crises weaken or destroy the pattern of restraints, the natural barbarism emerges behind the deceptive façade. Religion's most decisive social contribution is its effort to limit man's aggressiveness through love of God and neighbor.

A parallel effort of religion is aimed at man's self-righteousness. The Greek dramatists realized that at the core of the human tragedy was *hubris;* the author of Genesis stated the same truth in defining pride as the original sin. Religion seeks to limit this destructive force in human affairs by proclaiming every man's dependence upon God and by reminding him of his capacity for sin and error. It knows that the gulf between man and God must be bridged before the arrogant distinctions that man sets up against his fellows will crumble. Dostoevski's frightening alternative should haunt every nonbeliever: "If there is no God then I am God."

It cannot be claimed that religion at any time has adequately fulfilled all the demands of its calling. Nor will men agree to what extent the religions of the West have shaped those distinctive aspects of our culture, so demonstrably different from civilizations which have developed elsewhere. Yet one should give careful attention to the claims made by the distinguished historian who is Seth Low Professor Emeritus of Columbia University. In four lectures at Stanford University, Carleton Hayes traced the following as having emanated from the religious beliefs of the West: the dignity and importance of the individual; the concepts of liberty and natural rights; class mobility; the dignity of labor; the elevated position of woman; the plurality of authority and the division of power which gave birth to constitutional government; the emphasis on compassion and charitable work; and progressive dynamism based on the possibility of progress.[44] There is some support for this position when we consider the difficulty men have had in translating our Western political ideas of democracy, liberty, and equality to other cultures. It is clear that there is something in the soil of the West that encouraged their growth. It would be rash to exclude the fertilizing influence of Western religion as a factor.

In the contemporary context of American pluralism, what can and should the existing religious groups do to clarify the values of the community? It would seem that a prime task would be to deepen the American political faith in democracy. Democracy is a word of many meanings. It can be limited to "democratic institutions," the technique by which opinion shapes public decisions. These methods of voting and representation are vital to democracy. But if ever men were tempted to believe in the infallibility of majority vote, Nazi Germany and Fascist Italy have disillusioned them.

Beyond technique, democracy includes a set of propositions regarding the sanctity of the human person and the self-limita-

44. Carleton J. H. Hayes, *Christianity and Western Civilization* (Palo Alto: Stanford University Press, 1954).

tion of government. Historically, it is from these propositions that democracy has grown. Yet these concepts of man's equality, freedom, and worth are not demonstrable in a laboratory nor can they be proved from majority rule. They are articles of faith that can be reached only in the mind. Their roots lie, primarily, in the belief in a single God who is the Father of all and who created man in His image and made him responsible and free. To translate these beliefs into the political order took a long time and was achieved in part by men with religious convictions, like St. Thomas and Suárez. When they were finally applied in the eighteenth century, they were often defended by those who were not religiously orientated and opposed by many who were. But the thinkers of the Enlightenment did not invent the concepts that guided their political action. They were eclectic: they chose to retain the moral assumptions of their predecessors while many of them rejected the specifically religious. To them virtue and morality were of the highest importance for society and government, although the Biblical origins of this morality were considered outdated. They deserve our acclaim because they pushed the application of these principles beyond anything attempted by their forerunners, particularly in the fields of tolerance and criminology. But they no more started from scratch in their political thinking than their contemporaries did in the area of science.

What religion can do is to strengthen belief in the democratic propositions by emphasizing their moral foundations. This was made clear to the author of this paper during the Great Depression when I was frequently called upon to speak at meetings of workers who were groping toward union organization. These men and women had been numbed by economic catastrophe and were timid in the face of the powerful forces arrayed against their drive for unions of their own choosing. Experience showed that while references to the earlier struggles of labor in America were of some value, the most effective means was an exposition of human dignity in strictly religious terms. Again in the fight against segregation in the South, the remarkable success of Dr. Luther King is abundantly clear. This clergyman, a genuine folk hero of our epoch, makes no secret of the sources of his inspiration.

Few protest when religion is employed in behalf of such causes. More difficulty arises when religion is included in any public activity. Such a case involved the Supreme Court's decision outlawing a New York denominational prayer that school boards could use in public schools. The State Board of Regents had taken care to prevent offense to any group: the prayer was composed by leaders of the three faiths and no child was obliged to take part. When it was stricken down, most Catholics defended the prayer, most Jews approved the decision, Protestants divided.[45] Some of the disagreement stemmed from the ambiguity surrounding the scope of the decision. Justice Douglas in a concurring decision was clear: coming full around from his stand on the Zorach case, he expressed his willingness to exclude any manifestation of religion in public life. Justice Black, speaking for the majority, wrote an analysis of the evils of the imposition of the Book of Common Prayer in colonial America that seemed as relevant to this observer as a discussion of the pony express in the age of jet travel.

Some who believe in the value of religion argued that in this case little was lost as the eliminated prayer was not a true

45. An important minority of Jews supported the prayer as in the best traditions of their people. Reuben E. Gross, member of the National Board of the Union of Orthodox Jewish Congregations of America in so doing said that "the separation of church and state is a myth propagated by secularists in public life" (New York Times, Nov. 22, 1962, p. 40). Rabbi Menachem M. Schneerson wrote: "From every aspect of Jewish Law, it would appear clear that every Jew for whom the Torah (first five books of the Old Testament) is a guide is duty-bound to use every legal and constitutional means to see the majority decision of the Supreme Court on the Regents Prayer reversed." The rabbi pointed out that for many children the recitation of the Regents Prayer would offer the only opportunity to make some personal "contact with God every day." In the light of the attitude toward religion prevailing among some parents, "the hope expressed in some quarters that the banning of the Regents Prayer will somehow be compensated eventually by the introduction of more religion into the home is very doubtful." "With the exception of a small number of secularists and atheists, there is no person who in all conscience objects to a nondenominational prayer per se" (New York Times, Nov. 27, 1962, p. 25).

prayer at all. This is true in the sense that no religious body would employ it in church or synagogue. But the rubrics of a society are an indication of its values. Only the superficial miss the significance of symbols. The fact that each day the children stood for a moment to recognize their dependence upon God cannot be dismissed as unimportant. The daily salute to the flag can be shown to have an impact on the very children the prayer was supposed to leave untouched.

The reaction of the majority of American Catholics was a reflex both of their belief in the need to recognize God's primacy and of their experience in a country where they had come to expect the benevolent neutrality of the state. The shock arose from a feeling that this was not the America they had known, and if Justice Douglas's opinion were to prevail, it might not be the America they had loved. To some degree their concern transcended their immediate self-interest, for a smaller proportion of their children attend public school than in the case of the other religious bodies. But it may be true that they have not thought through all the implications of a pluralist society, particularly in reference to the small minority which objects to any reference to God in public forum. There is even a possibility that American Catholics may have to learn, as have the Jews in so many areas, how to live in a society which does not reflect their values. This would be a new experience for them in America for even in their earlier experience here the Protestant-dominated culture had standards they could understand. If an unqualified observer may hazard a prediction: I do not think that Catholics will face this problem in the forseeable future as religious feeling is still deeply imbedded in the people; were they to have to, I suspect that they would do it with the flexibility that their history in America suggests.

A second major question that arouses serious controversy must be briefly treated. During the era of the Protestant control of American culture many states passed legislation whose purpose was to reinforce the moral code as the Protestant then viewed it. In none of these efforts did the Catholic minority play a role. In some of them, as in Prohibition and in laws forbidding games of chance and Sunday recreation, the Catholics were in hearty opposition. Many of these laws have fallen into disuse or have been repealed. But in some states with a large Catholic population, moves to rescind legislation on providing information on contraceptives or on making divorce more accessible have met with Catholic opposition. When the proposals are directed toward removing obstacles to abortion, euthanasia, or sterilization, Catholic opposition is even stiffer.

In all these cases Catholics base their position on Natural Right principles. In the matter of abortion they maintain the stand that the unborn child is a human being who has the same God-given right to life as has any other person. As for euthanasia they take the ground that no man has the right to usurp God's role by deciding who should live and who should die. Not only does the sick person retain his right to life, but there is the danger that the decision to eliminate him will be influenced by subjective factors, such as the inconvenience he causes or the cost of his maintenance. The Catholic reaction to the practice of the Virginia county which sterilized its relief clients, mainly Negro, was equally unfavorable. Again, Catholics believed that no person should be deprived of his right to procreate his kind in return for a community pittance, to which as a member of that community he has a just title; that it was unjust to ask him to undergo a permanent deprivation to meet a temporary economic need; and that as a majority of those sterilized were Negroes, there was a strong possibility of snobbery, if not of racial discrimination. That this policy was proposed in an affluent America indicated that the basic tenet of care for the unfortunate, so strenuously maintained by Western religion since the time of Moses, was being seriously eroded.

Behind these positions, and many others, is the Catholic belief in an objective moral law. This was cogently stated by Pope John XXIII in the encyclical *Mater et Magistra:* There is "no such thing as a free world unless there is a code of morality that is transcendent, absolute, universal, equally binding upon all."[46] This has been the prevailing attitude of Western thought, and its strength derived from its twofold source in the majority of Greek philosophers and in all the Hebrew religious leaders. So powerful has it been in our history that it has been contended that the two fundamental assumptions of American culture at the dawn of the twentieth century were belief in progress and in the reality of a universal moral law with man's consequent responsibility to it. Since that time moral relativism has risen sharply.

One of the more distinguished spokesmen for the relativist point of view has declared that a democratic community has no right to legislate against sin. "One man's sin may be another man's duty and a third man's bliss." He then makes an important distinction:

> It is one thing to advocate prohibition and a ban against national lotteries on the ground that such legislation furthers the public welfare.
> But it is something else again to propose that gambling and the consumption of liquor should be forbidden by law because they are sinful according to some religious dogmas. . . .
> A democratic community . . . cannot recognize the category of sin, legislate against it and punish those for whom the proscribed action is not sinful.[47]

Catholics would enthusiastically support this distinction. I suspect that even the Protestants who advocated the prohibition of liquor and gambling would declare that they were operating in the interest of the public welfare. Certainly Catholics do when they oppose relaxation of laws against such things as "mercy killing." This is not a crusade against "sin" but a contention that if one person could legally kill a man on the ground that he was maimed or ill or "unfit," the whole structure of human life would be endangered and society

46. *America*, Vol. 105, No. 18, July, 1961, p. 565.
47. Professor Sidney Hook of New York University, *New York Times*, Nov. 21, 1962.

itself inperiled. Man has attained a high regard for the sacredness of human life with great effort; his present hold on human dignity is precarious. To give legal sanction to a form of killing or maiming would weaken the key concepts of our civilization.

Catholics would be practically unanimous on the above issues and they would find strong support outside their communion. There is a different situation where the majority of Americans have abandoned a position they have once held and which they have written into legislation. Such an instance would be the anticontraceptive laws of Connecticut. While the majority of Catholics would support the official position of the Church that the use of these devices is an interference with a natural and sacred process of life-formation, there would be division on the desirability of supporting this by legislation in the current climate of opinion. Those who believe that considerations of the common good justify the removal of such legislation quote St. Thomas's distinction between law and morality:

> Now human law is laid down for the multitude, the major part of which is composed of men not perfected by virtue. Consequently, all and every vice, from which virtuous men abstain, is not prohibited by human law, but only the gravest vicious actions, from which it is possible for the major part of the multitude to abstain, and mainly those —like homicide, theft, etc.—which are harmful to others, and without the prohibition of which human society could not be preserved.[48]

There is a good deal of flux in the non-Catholic American community on these basic moral issues. The Nazi practice of legally condemning innocent people to the gas chamber and to the sterilization ward shocked those who have argued that there is no higher law than the positive enactment of the legislator. In all such crises men instinctively appeal against the injustice of the human law to the higher moral principle.

48. *Summa Theologica*, i-ii, 96, 2.

This was done on an international scale in the Nuremberg trials. There is some indication that the impact of our experience with totalitarian legislation is forcing a reexamination among students of law on the issue of the relation between law and morality.

Historically the conflict on the relation between religion and culture has centered in education. This is natural, for all realize that the future form of culture will depend on the nature of the instruction given to the young. In every country where the modern *Kulturkampf* has been waged—France is the classic example—[49] education has been the core of the struggle. In each country the terrain has been different. In all it begins in the realm of the abstract and arrives at the practical: the issue of the right of the religiously orientated school to claim some measure of public support.

In the United States, as elsewhere, education was once in private, and generally religious, hands. It was a pragmatic reason which moved our government to promote public education: the flood of immigrants was placing an intolerable burden upon the existing private system at the time when the need for universal education was becoming more apparent. This move into the field of education fitted the American policy of taking over functions only where necessary, that is, where they were being inadequately performed by nongovernmental agencies. Public education was not proclaimed to be something inherent in democratic government, nor did the government propose to preempt the field of education, any more than it later attempted to drive from the welfare field those voluntary agencies which wished to serve the public good. The government simply intended to fill a need by coexisting with the established voluntary groups. It continued to maintain as a matter of principle that the parents had a prior right to educate their children and to determine the kind of education they were to receive.

49. Evelyn M. Acomb, *The French Laic Laws* (New York: Columbia University Press, 1941).

Almost at once the issue of state aid to the preexisting independent schools arose. The New York State law of 1812 had distributed tax funds to private and religious as well as public schools. In New York City, the latter were supervised by a private educational corporation known as the Free School Society, later as the Public School Society. It was this organization which launched a drive for monopoly when in 1822 it attacked the application of the Bethel Baptist Church for public aid for its parish school. Methodists, Episcopalians, Dutch Reformed and Catholics supported the Baptists, but their case was lost in the courts. In 1842 when Catholics, a Jewish synagogue, and a Scottish Presbyterian congregation made a similar plea a majority of the Protestants were in opposition. The reason for the change of view was that the bulk of the arriving immigrants were Catholic, and the Protestants came to the conviction that their cause could best be served in schools with a general Christian flavor. In the controversy there is no hint that the public schools won acceptance because they were irreligious, which they were not, but because they solved a Protestant problem.[50] There was a curious consequence to these developments. The initial Catholic effort to expand their school system came as a response to the Protestant character of the public schools of that day; the more recent expansion by Catholics and other religious groups has occurred in proportion to and precisely in those areas where religion of a general Protestant sort has been progressively excluded from the public school.

The public school went on to deserve a privileged place in the American tradition because of its success in bringing the children of the immigrant into cultural unity with his fellow Americans. Some educators today suggest that it too thoroughly eliminated the foreign languages and customs that the

50. Richard J. Gobel, *Public Funds for Catholic and Private Schools* (Washington: Catholic University Press, 1937). The Protestant position was made easier because the major denominations in America had been the dissenting sects in Europe: Francis X. Curran, *The Churches and the Schools* (Chicago: Loyola University Press, 1944), pp. 1ff.; Edwin H. Riaux, *Christianity and American Education*, San Antonio, 1949; pp. 2off.

newcomers brought with them; but this was inevitable. Some have advanced the view that since the process of Americanization has been practically concluded and the present need is for excellence in education, the contemporary role of the public school is less obvious. This is not the view of the author of this paper. The public school has not only won a hallowed place in American life; it will continue to be the vehicle chosen by the majority of American parents for the education of their children.

There is a more difficult question involving the contemporary public school. Unquestionably it was once religious in the sense defined above. Is it today? All depends on definition. Every school has a commitment to some ultimate beliefs. Even the attempt at neutrality cannot eliminate from teaching a judgment on the meaning of life, the nature of man, the reality of God, the structure of human knowledge, and the functions of human society. Justice Black would certainly concur here, for in the majority opinion in *Torcaso* vs. *Watkins* (1961) he gave the broadest definition to religion when he specifically termed secular humanism as a religion. He could find some support in common experience: it would be difficult to teach economics without passing some judgment on Marxian determinism; if the verdict be unfavorable, it would be hard to make it without reference to some view of man's nature. The human mind is not a receptacle with compartments. It is alive and wants to know "why." An education would be incomplete if it did not explore the deeper meanings. To the Jew or Christian these lead to God.

It would seem that if God exists, He cannot be ignored in education. If there be a God, He is the central reality in the universe and should be in education. This is the firm belief of a large number of Americans who, as a consequence, cannot accept a school which is not God-centered. Justice Jackson showed some appreciation of this view in his concurring opinion in the McCollum case:

I think it remains to be demonstrated whether it is possible, even if desirable, to comply with such demands as plaintiff's completely to violate and cast out of secular education all that some people may reasonably regard as religious instruction. . . . The fact is that, for good or ill, nearly everything in our culture worth transmitting, everything which gives meaning to life is saturated with religious influences, derived from paganism, Judaism, Christianity—both Catholic and Protestant—and other faiths accepted by a large part of the world's peoples. One can hardly respect a system of education that would leave the student wholly ignorant of the currents of religious thought that move the world society, for a part in which he is being prepared.[51]

Judaism and Christianity not merely affirm God's existence and his centrality; they believe that God has spoken to man in the Old and New Testaments. To them religion is not a vague feeling but a body of doctrine that has been made explicit in terms of God's word to man. To one who believes this profoundly, it becomes a matter of conscience that religion become an integral part of teaching. This was succinctly put in a resolution accepted by a panel of the World Conference of Jewish Organizations meeting in Jerusalem:

The Jewish youth who receives a full Jewish and secular education is a more integrated person and thereby a more useful citizen.[52]

Obviously not all agree. Some argue that religion can be taught successfully in the Church, synagogue, or home as a supplement to formal education. No one would question the value of these additives which have given us the Sunday and Sabbath school and the released time program. But a growing number of Americans are not convinced that these are adequate and would support the conclusion of Rabbi Seymour Siegel, Assistant Professor of Theology at the Jewish Theological Seminary:

51. *McCollum* v. *Board of Education,* 333 U.S. 203, (1948).
52. *New York Times,* Aug. 15, 1962.

## A Catholic View of Contemporary Conflict

It is difficult to sustain an argument which separates the religious from the secular. It is impossible to teach any subject in the curriculum without reference to religion. . . . The disproportionate amount of time which is spent in the school in relation to other educational institutions (home, church, etc.) usually results in the school influencing the church and synagogue than vice versa. If the child is habituated to thinking in naturalistic terms, it is difficult to combat the way of thinking in supplementary education.[53]

This is the view of the American bishops who wrote in their letter of November 14, 1947:

In the rearing of children and the forming of youth, omission is as effective as positive statement. A philosophy of education which omits God, necessarily draws a plan of life in which either God has no place or is a strictly private concern of man.[54]

Finally, Jew and Christian believe that God has given man a Law which concerns all man's dealings with nature and with other men. Those who accept this in conscience may well fear that the gap in the teaching between the home and the school may become so wide that it cannot be bridged by the good will of the parents.

The rights of parents with these convictions have been supported throughout our constitutional history. The classic locus is the unanimous decision of the Supreme Court in the Oregon case, June 1, 1925. In striking down a statute that would have required all students to attend state schools, the court held:

The fundamental theory of liberty upon which all governments in this Union repose excludes any general power of the State to standardize its children by forcing them

53. *America*, Vol. 107, No. 25, Sept. 22, 1962, p. 777. It is true that the home and the religious community have the primary responsibility for moral education, but the school should contribute the intellectual foundation of moral life: *The Education of Man: The Educational Philosophy of Jacques Maritain*, Donald and Idella Gallagher, eds. (Garden City: Doubleday, 1962), pp. 103-128.
54. Raphael M. Huber, *Our Bishops Speak* (Milwaukee: Bruce Publishing Co., 1952), pp. 137-144.

to accept instruction from public teachers only. The child is not the mere creature of the State; those who nurture him and direct his destiny have the right, coupled with the high duty, to recognize and prepare him for additional obligations.[55]

The principle is so deeply rooted in democratic practice that it was incorporated in similar terms in the United Nations Universal Declaration of Human Rights. In proclaiming the primary right of the parents in educational matters both our own government and the world body recognize that they enter the educational process in order to aid the parents, not to deny them their rights. In this, as in other areas where rights are involved, the government acts with the consent of the governed. This was the primary purpose of the Bill of Rights: to protect the individual from the government where his essential prerogatives are involved. It is most instructive to compare this democratic approach with the theory and universal practice of totalitarian governments who sweep aside both rights of parents and independent schools and establish a monopoly over the instruction of the young.

If we analyze the relation of government to education in the contemporary world, we will arrive at this equation: a pluralist society, a pluralist education; a monopolistic society, a monopolistic education. It is the knowledge that the American people abhor a monopoly, particularly a governmental monopoly, that encourages the proponents of the independent school. Americans would be nearly unanimous in opposing government monopoly in business. They can be trusted to reject a more dangerous monopoly in education. Their common sense tells them that competition, which is recognized as helpful in most fields, is useful here as well.

The American political experiment rests on the concept of limited government, which fits naturally into the structure of pluralist education. Our government should not strive for monopolistic education if for no other reason than that dif-

55. *Pierce* vs. *the Society of Sisters*, 45 U.S. 571 (1925), reaffirmed in *Price* vs. *Massachusetts*, 64 U.S. 438 (1944).

111

ferent segments of our pluralist society have different educational needs. Millions of American parents and children are Protestants, Catholics, and Jews, and the state cannot compel them to act as though they were not such during the process of their learning. The state should provide "public" education in the exact sense: an education that should meet the needs and the aspirations of the whole body of the public. This would require that it provide a "neutral" or "nonreligious" education for those who want it and a religious education for any part of the population who prefer this type. This would be a genuine pluralism, not its shadow.

Jacques Maritain argues, in a way that should appeal to all who examine the meaning of democracy, that a democratic state can only teach in its broad outlines the consensus which lies at the base of political society. It cannot impose a philosophical or religious explanation without violating its democratic principles. But these propositions cannot be, and are not, in fact, left as abstractions. If they were, they would have little impact on the minds of the citizens. Accordingly a democratic state must rely on the various religious bodies and different schools of thought to put flesh and blood on the skeleton of the consensus:

> . . . It would be sheer illusion to think that the democratic charter could be efficiently taught if it were separated from the roots which gave it consistence and vigor in the minds of each one, and if it were reduced to a series of abstract formulas—bookish, bloodless, and cut off from life. Those who teach the democratic charter must believe in it, and stake on it their personal convictions, their consciences, and the depths of their moral life. They must therefore explain and justify its articles in the light of the philosophy or religion to which they cling and which quickens their belief in the common charter.[56]

These very principles should demand that democratic societies exercise care when they enter the field of education. By accepting the obligation to teach, the state has logically

56. Jacques Maritain, *Man and the State* (Chicago: Chicago University Press, 1951), p. 121.

become involved in many aspects of their students' well-being: their health and medical care, their recreation, their moral habits and psychological guidance. Thus the entire development of the child has become the function of governmental agencies, and these have the power and the wealth of the community behind them. They certainly perform beneficent services. Yet their activities must come within the purview of Justice Brennan's warning before the National Council of the Social Sciences that the vigilance needed "to prevent government from whittling away the rights of the individual was never greater than it is today."[57]

The danger is greater still in education, which is one of the few fields in which democratic governments have found it necessary to use compulsion to obtain universal compliance. It is not unfair to compare the American government's sensitivity to the religious rights of the individual who serves in its armed forces with the sensitivity we should expect from it in education, for these are the two major areas affecting the lives of its citizens where the compulsive factor is directly employed. In the military service the government accepts religion as a fact of life. It is considered just to compel a man to serve his country, but not to give up his religion. So the government at its expense provides chaplains and the materials they need to operate—chapels, books, equipment—not to serve the churches or synagogue, but to serve the soldier. The American tradition does not see this as governmental aid to religion, but as religion's aid to government. There is a recognition on the part of the military that it has a mission to make available religion and morality which it is itself not equipped to provide.

That this attitude is not carried over to education requires no demonstration. On the contrary, it provokes the kind of explosive utterance made by Kenneth W. Greenawalt, a lawyer for the American Civil Liberties Union: "I believe the wall of separation [between church and state] must be kept im-

57. *New York Times,* Nov. 25, 1962, p. 73.

pregnable. . . . There is no place for compromise or degrees of separation. Separation means separation, not something less. . . . The 'child-benefit theory' is the greatest menace today to the constitutional separation of church and state."[58]

If one had not seen the deadly seriousness of those who propound such views, one might dismiss statements of this sort as rhetoric. Here is an example of a person deciding for himself what is meant by the phrase, "separation of church and state," erecting his interpretation into a constitutional dogma, and proceeding to denounce all deviations from his position as constitutionally unacceptable. It is the use of slogans for rational argument. It is irrelevant that there is no constitutional evidence for this interpretation from the time our national document was written till now, if we except a few isolated opinions of individual justices of the Court which in the broadest extension of the term do not qualify as "constitutional." What such a statement does in effect is to urge the separation of *my* government from *your* church. More shocking is the sentence that the consideration of benefit to the child in education has become a menace. Here I find myself in the chill presence of the totalitarian mind which is oblivious to the value of the human person which is the seedbed of democracy.

What is difficult to understand is why the field of education should be separated from the usual procedures of democratic government. The American people have been presented with a variety of proposals for governmental action in the field of medical care. Some support an advanced program; some would have none at all. But in the whole spectrum of opinion on this question, there is not a single advocate of a theory that would require a patient to see a particular doctor.

58. *New York Times*, Nov. 21, 1962. For a brief statement that the denial of aid to religious schools is discriminatory, see Wilbur G. Katz, *The Case for Religious Liberty*, pp. 108-115, in *Religion in America*, ed. John Cogley (New York: Meridian Books, 1958). To the author the prohibition against establishment was an instrumental principle to remove restraints upon religious liberty: ". . . strict separation of church and state would involve hostility to religion and intolerable curtailment of religious freedom" (p. 98). See also the important symposium, "Religious Freedom in America," in *Cross Currents*, Vol. XIII, # 1, Winter 1963, pp. 3-75.

The very idea is abhorent, for we are committed to the notion of a sacred relation between patient and doctor.

As a people we are equally devoted to the idea of a sacred relation between parent and child. Certainly we profess the right of the parent to choose the form of education for his child as solemnly as we honor the patient's right to choose his doctor. But in the case of education we are content with the statement of principle. We are not ready to concede the means that are necessary to implement it. This is the core of the problem of public aid to the independent school. We freely grant any citizen the right to send his child to a school of his own choosing where religion is an explicit part of the curriculum. We realize that this is the type of education his conscience demands. We know that a pluralistic society cannot provide this type in goverment-sponsored schools. Yet while we declare that this is a matter of right, we continue to regard the exercise of this right as a luxury that concerns no one but himself. Is this not like granting a man the right to eat, but denying him food?

An illustration may help: in my community there is a religious elementary school with 570 pupils in a modern building and with a level of secular instruction that is regarded as the equal of any in the area. The community adjoins the United States Military Academy at West Point and 170 of these pupils are children of the military personnel on the post. The parents of the rest live in the town and the vast majority of them are either military people or civilian workers at West Point. The Federal Government provides an elementary school on the Academy grounds. It pays for all students it sends to the town's high school, and because of the civilian workers and military personnel in the town, it pays a share of the community's school budget. These same public schools all receive their proportion of state taxes and impose local levies on all citizens. Those who send their children to the religious school pay their share of school taxes on all three levels of government. They also carry all the other burdens of citizenship—in this case obviously so, because many wear the uniform. They have the right, all say, to choose their type of education. But let them use it if they can. It is significant that the Attorney General, Robert Kennedy, had filed a brief in the name of the government against the school boards of Prince George County, Virginia, on the score that the country's schools treated some servicemen's children as inferior. "It is even more incongruous," said the Justice Department's brief, "that these systems are supported by public funds, contributed in part by the fathers of these children." Could not the same words be applied to the servicemen in the West Point area who use their right to send their children to a religiously orientated school?

The most cherished principle in American culture is equality. Tocqueville was so impressed by its vigor in America that to him equality was synonymous with democracy. Gunnar Myrdal has shown that even when we deny equality of treatment to our Negro citizens, we are haunted by a sense of betrayal. Yet when refugees from the Cuba of Castro inundated the schools of the Miami area, we made no effort to treat them equally. A high proportion of them were Catholics who wished to send their children to religious schools. The children were accepted to the limit possible, so both religious and public schools were equally burdened. But the local school boards successfully appealed to the national government for relief in the form of special funds; for identically the same service to the nation and to humanity the religious schools could not.

Such situations, and they are repeated on a national pattern, deserve to be taken seriously. When Catholics, and those Protestant and Jewish minorities who operate such schools, appeal to American public opinion, they are seeking relief from a condition which they regard as discriminatory. They ask their fellow citizens to reflect if these schools are not public schools in the true sense. Certainly they correspond to a public need, if each group is to be accorded full religious liberty. They fulfill a public role in providing a general education of a quality equal to that of government supported schools, and they train their students adequately in the responsibilities of citizenship. The religious schools follow the same general curriculum, are subject to the same criteria, and their diplomas have the same value as those issued by state supported schools.

In asking government to aid these schools they are seeking something that is common in other fields. Government already aids libraries and museums under private control when it finds that they fulfill a public purpose. It grants subsidies to airlines and steamship companies when it believes that their maintenance is in the public interest. It finds ways to aid a world's fair when it believes the image of America should be reflected therein. It uses my tax funds for these purposes even though I may never visit a museum, ride an airplane, or patronize a world's fair. It acts simply on what it considers the broad public interest. The decisive point in state aid to independent schools is: do these schools serve a public purpose, or is it desirable in America to set up a monopolistic school system under governmental control against the wishes and conscience of a substantial minority of its citizens?

When President Kennedy proposed federal funds for education, he emphasized that the American children needed and deserved the best possible education to fit them for the world that is being shaped by the advancing technology of today. One cannot ignore in this argument the millions of Americans who will be formed in the religious schools of our country. We are beginning to learn that we cannot, in justice or in self-interest, spurn the talents and skills of our Negro citizens; we have still to learn that we cannot pass over those who in conscience choose religiously orientated schools. For what concerns those who run these schools and those who choose them for their children is the mounting cost of providing the type of education that is needed today. The transition from the simple material of yesteryear to the complicated educational equipment of the present is the decisive factor in raising the issue of state aid. Those who are responsible for these schools —it was particularly clear in the case of the Jewish day schools—entered the arena only when they believed that the survival of their institutions was at stake. That these fears were not groundless is evident in the dramatic shift on the college level from the private to the public institution. In 1950 it was estimated that half of the college students of the country were in schools under private auspices. By 1980 it is expected that the proportion may be 20 percent in the private colleges, 80 percent in the public. While Harvard will survive —and perhaps even continue to supply the leadership in our national government—the outlook for many excellent small liberal arts colleges is dim. They simply cannot compete with an ever-increasing volume of money which the government collects from all of its citizens but allocates selectively.

This would be the time in our history for Americans to ask themselves some stern questions. Do we really want to cripple or snuff out the independent schools which have contributed so generously to the American development? Or would it be in the interest of all to maintain them at least in a semi-independent status in the face of the continuing enlargement of governmental power? Further, do we really believe that if we removed all references to God from public institutions that we would thereupon enter upon a regime of sweetness and light in which we would all respect each other and guard each other's rights? Would we really be satisfied to have all our moral judgments formed by our mass media, which in addition to some good music, sports, and news, brings "a superficially pleasurable but stultifying collection of myths, illusions, and wishful thinking"? Do we really believe that a comic strip is a better vehicle for instructing youth than the story of David or the parable of the Good Samaritan? In our other-directed society would it be ultimately profitable to remove from the public forum those inspirations which derive from religious faith and put our trust and our sacred rights into the hands of those who provide the tranquilizers of our popular culture?

Even if we could answer these questions, we would not necessarily solve all the problems that arise from our pluralistic society. But posing them seriously might help us decide what kind of America we want, for in the long run that is the kind of an America we will have. For my part I am haunted by the question which a beloved friend, the late Franz Neumann, used to insist upon in his graduate classes in Columbia: to what degree was the Nazi thing a product of specifically German history and to what degree did it come from the leveling and conformist tendencies of modern technological society? Concretely, how did the average well meaning German turn his back on the concentration camp and gas chamber without questioning the actions of his government? The real problem is not the Storm Trooper. Any society can produce the bully, the sadist, the seeker after power. The frightening reality was the spiritual vacuum, the absence of deep moral conviction about human dignity and the natural law. Surely there were many extenuating circumstances as the Germans had been defeated in war and had suffered economic collapse. But what else was involved?

On the positive side the limits of this essay will allow only a few modest suggestions. Some feel that we are now involved in an American version of the *Kulturkampf*, though one fought with words and with legal briefs. Is there any common ground that we could find that would make possible a combined constructive contribution to American culture?

It would seem that the first step would be to accept the reality of Herberg's triad of Protestant, Catholic, and Jew, with due allowance for those who are none of these. This would involve more than recognizing the other's presence. It would mean accepting the other's right to be there and his general good intentions. It is obvious that any religious group in any forseeable future will remain a permanent minority in American life. Accordingly, civic peace will depend on our capacity to develop mutual trust. The basis for this trust must be the fact that the condition for survival for any religious group in America is *guaranteed* freedom. For all of them can continue to live in a secular state, as long as it does not become a secularistic state with an antireligious ideology.

But more than peaceful coexistence is necessary if America is to be genuinely enriched. It would be possible to extract from the religious tradition, common to us all, those ideals which have universal appeal and application. Lenin remarked that "without revolutionary theory, there can be no revolutionary action." Certainly it has become apparent that democratic action is ineffective without the stiffening of principle. All religious groups in America affirm the principles that are needed to underpin our democratic structure: the primacy of man in creation which derives from his God-bestowed intelligence and freedom; the primacy of the moral and the spiritual in human concerns; the dignity and worth of every human being; the collateral principle of his responsibility to, and his need to recognize, an objective moral code. This is the rich treasure of the American religious heritage. It belongs to us all. Our nation and our world have need of it now. It may appear curious to posterity that at this central point in history the three great religious bodies in America spent their time wrangling about a children's morning prayer. Maimonides, Aquinas, and Calvin would have been puzzled.

On the most divisive issue among us—that of public aid to independent education—a calm study of the procedures in other democratic countries should calm fears and renew intelligent discussion. Whenever everyone is out of step but Johnny, it behooves Johhny to look at his own feet. In nearly every other nation with principles like our own, government has entered into partnership with religious groups in the matter of primary interest to all—the education of youth. While we will find our own solution, the experience of our peers should help.

# CHAPTER THREE

# AMERICA
# IS
# DIFFERENT

by Arthur Hertzberg

*"Congress shall make no law respecting an establishment of religion, or prohibiting the free exercise thereof."*

## I

The First Amendment to the Constitution of the United States was not a direct revelation from heaven. The separation of church and state in this country was devised by men; it was voted into law by legislatures which did not consist of cloistered monks or abstract philosophers. Behind this act there lay the historic experience of the thirteen colonies, the immediate situation at the time when this country was founded, and the new outlook on life and religion which animated such typically eighteenth century intellectuals as Jefferson and Madison. We cannot therefore understand what the Founding

Fathers intended merely by parsing every word of the text of the First Amendment, or by writing interpretative legalistic briefs, no matter how brilliant. This act grew from life; its immediate causes were a political revolution and a change in spiritual outlook; and it was clearly intended to represent more than a set of ground rules about the relationship between two powerful institutions, the state and the church. In the great age when the grooves were cut for the new society, the First Amendment set out the American version of the response to perhaps the most fundamental of all questions, the polarity between religion and society.

As Justice Jackson observed in a famous dissent, conflicting passions tend to obscure the meaning of the First Amendment: "This policy of our Federal Constitution has never been wholly pleasing to most religious groups. They all are quick to invoke its protection; they all are irked when they feel its restraints."[1] He could well have added that in argument each group is prone to maintain not that the amendment should be changed, but that it really meant, from the beginning, what each group finds convenient and useful at that particular moment. Let us, therefore, try to fix what the First Amendment really did mean. For what ideas did it speak? To what situation was it addressed? What kind of future did its framers envision for the new nation?

Intellectually, the separation of church and state in America has two roots, in the radical Protestantism of Roger Williams and in both the criticisms and affirmations about religion that were the common coin of the eighteenth century Enlightenment. Williams had gone out into the wilderness to found Rhode Island in order to escape repression in Massachusetts, where the dominant Puritans were using civil power against religious nonconformists. He held that constraint of any sort

---

1. This quotation is from his dissent in 1946 in the *Everson* case. The majority, five to four, upheld the right of New Jersey to pay the bus fare of all children going to school, including those who were attending Catholic parochial schools. Supreme Court of the United States, October Term, 1946, No. 52.

in matters of spiritual faith was beyond the inherent powers of civil magistrates. In the priesthood of all believers each man had to find his own way to salvation. An established church meant somnolence even for truth, and too frequently it lent itself to the triumph of error. Only absolute freedom for all religious views could leave open the channels of grace and lead to the development of a true Christian commonwealth. Williams, hence, affirmed not only the right of all kinds of Christians to their various beliefs. He went so far, in all logic, as to insist that all other religions had to be equally free, and equally disestablished and separate from the state.[2]

These views certainly make Roger Williams the direct American ancestor of the separation of church and state, but we must be careful to distinguish between his position and any parallel notions about dividing religion from society. It was basic to the whole of Williams's outlook to deny that human life is divided into two realms of authority, the spiritual and the temporal. This distinction came from medieval Catholic thought; it was being used in his time in England to defend Charles I as king by divine right. As a political revolutionary Williams could not accept the notion that any existing civil order was grounded in immutable right. In his view the state was an instrument created by compact for limited purposes. It was a convenient arrangement, not an end in itself. As a

2. "(1) God requireth not an uniformity of Religion to be inacted and inforced in any civil state; which inforced uniformity (sooner or later) is the greatest occasion of civill Warre, ravishing of conscience, persecution of Christ Jesus in his servants, and of the hypocrisie and destruction of millions of souls. . . . (2) It is the will and command of God, that . . . a permission of the most Paganish, Jewish, Turkish, or Antichristian consciences and worships, bee granted to all men in all Nations and Countries: and they are onely to bee fought against with that Sword which is onely (in Soule matters) able to conquer, to wit, the Sword of Gods Spirit, the Word of God. (3) True civility and Christianity may both flourish in a state or Kingdome, notwithstanding the permission of divers and contrary consciences, either of Jew or Gentile." *The Bloody Tenent of Persecution for Cause of Conscience* (1644), quoted in Vernon L. Parrington, *Main Currents in American Thought* (New York: Harcourt, 1927), Vol. I, p. 71. See also Leo Pfeffer, *Church, State and Freedom* (Boston: Beacon, 1953), pp. 75-78.

serious Christian, and a mystical one, Williams was certain that the true business of life was not the running of the commonwealth or the organization of an effective civil polity but the quest for grace and salvation. He limited the realms of the state and the civil order very severely in order to get them out of the way of the individual. They were to be relegated to their proper humble and neutral role as a reduced enclave in human culture. Neither the state nor society had any sacred character, or real importance, for both were to be regarded as constantly under spiritual judgment. Roger Williams disestablished religion in order to free it for its proper task, to become coextensive with culture.

In the seventeenth century, or the eighteenth of Jefferson and Madison, it was imaginable that the state could be defined as a minimal kind of arrangement and kept from impinging on most of life. In colonial America, and in the United States created by the authors of the Constitution, it seemed indubitable that this country would represent an overwhelmingly Christian, indeed a Protestant, population and ethos. Williams's plea for full freedom for all religions was both noble and notable, but it was clear that he was not guilty of "indifferentism," that is, of the view that one religion is as good as another or that no religion is as good as any. Christianity was, to him, the true faith. The purpose of freedom for all religions was to expedite the day when all mankind would perceive its truth.

The main thrust of the Enlightenment, the other source of the First Amendment, was in the opposite direction—that spiritual revolution turned the focus of man's concern away from his eternal salvation to the ordering of his life, and that of society, in this world. Its purpose, contrary to Roger Williams, was not to free religion from social restraint but to protect society from the squabbling sects.

Some of the intellectual leaders of the Enlightenment did sincerely believe in the superior truth of Christianity, but the total impact of the new thinking was in the negative. Voltaire's famous attacks on the Bible and on the priesthood led to the conclusion that Western religion was no better, indeed perhaps worse, than some others. A society reordered by reason would forbid the sects to quarrel or to oppress each other. At the root of all religions, in the view of Rousseau (when he was not being the prophet of a new totalitarian state religion of patriotism), there was an underlying unity in natural religion which all men could know if they would but follow right reason and true instinct. They would be made to discover that each sect represented a variant set of symbols and myths, which men could continue to use and accept, provided they did it peacefully and without any attempt to push their own private values on others. The religious duty common to all men is the acknowledgment of a Supreme Being to whom they all owe homage. In sum, the Enlightenment set out to incarnate its God of reason in a reasonable society and to teach the religions the truth about themselves that they did not yet know and a new way to behave in the light of that truth.

From such thinking it was but a short step to positing reason, good citizenship and the worship of the Supreme Being as the source and support of a new progressive world order. At the height of the French Revolution the *Etre Suprême* was at first worshiped in elaborately staged rituals in which priests, ministers, and rabbis participated together in enforced fraternity. Soon, however, in the midst of the Terror, the cathedral of Notre Dame was turned into a temple of reason, along with some buildings of other faiths, including several synagogues. Divinely sanctioned patriotism thus became the counterfaith to the older dispensations. In America events never went that far, but the Enlightenment did bequeath to the framers of the First Amendment something of its testiness with the traditional faiths, and of its desire to make of them a small private enclave in the larger, freer new life. The pervasive American notion that religion, generically and through its various sects, is the support of society rather than its judge is a conservative recension of the Jacobin outlook.

The arguments of James Madison's *Memorial and Remonstrance* of 1785 are often quoted as the authoritative expression of what was in the mind of the future author of the First Amendment. Indeed, the Supreme Court minority in the *Everson* case and the majority in the recent Regents Prayer decision were both at great pains to enlist this paper by Madison as the chief proof text for their views. With much of his reasoning coming from Roger Williams, Madison was indeed very firm in his emphasis on the superiority of Christianity; he pleaded for disestablishment as the greatest good that could come to the true faith. Nonetheless something of the outlook of the Enlightenment does come through among his arguments against an establishment of religion: "Because, it will destroy that moderation and harmony which the forbearance of our laws to intermeddle with Religion, has produced amongst its several sects. Torrents of blood have been spilt in the old world, by vain attempts of the secular arm to extinguish Religious discord, by proscribing all difference in Religious opinions. Time has at length revealed the true remedy. Every relaxation of narrow and rigorous policy, wherever it has been tried has been found to assuage the disease. The American Theatre has exhibited proofs, that equal and compleat liberty, if it does not wholly eradicate it, sufficiently destroys its malignant influence on the health and prosperity of the State. If with the salutary effects of this system under our own eyes, we begin to contract the bonds of Religious freedom, we know no name that will too severely reproach our folly."

The impact of the Enlightenment on Thomas Jefferson's views on religion was greater and more evident. His distaste for all the organized sects, and their priesthoods, was pure Voltaire.[3] He did not stop at criticizing Christianity or its

3. "I am not afraid of the priests. They have tried upon me all their various batteries, of pious whining, hypocritical canting, lying and slander-

various denominations. Even the figure of Jesus himself, as he is depicted in the New Testament, was discussed on the presumption that Jefferson's own modern thought was superior.[4] In its full expression, much of this stance represents the later Jefferson, during and after his Presidency; it is to that later stage of his life that we owe the famous phrase about the "wall of separation" between church and state, which has so often been invoked as the authoritative commentary on the First Amendment. The younger Jefferson, however, in the years contemporary with his authorship of the Virginia bill for religious liberty, was already just as critical of the various faiths: "Difference of opinion is advantageous in religion. The several sects perform the office of *censor morum* over each other."[5]

The tension between radical Protestant faith and the Enlightenment as the two intellectual sources of separation of church and state is best illustrated today in the changing mind

---

ing, without being able to give me one moment of pain. I have contemplated their order from the Magi of the East to the Saints of the West, and I have found no difference of character, but of more or less caution, in proportion to their information or ignorance of those on whom their interested duperies were to be plaid off. Their sway in New England is indeed formidable. No mind beyond mediocrity dares there to develop itself." Quoted from Saul K. Padover, *Thomas Jefferson on Democracy* (New York: Mentor Books 1946), p. 122.

4. "It is not to be understood that I am with him [Jesus] in all his doctrines. I am a Materialist; he takes the side of Spiritualism; he preaches the efficacy of repentance towards forgiveness of sin; I require a counterpoise of good works to redeem it, etc. It is the innocence of his character, the purity and sublimity of his moral precepts, the eloquence of his inculcations, the beauty of the apologues in which he conveys them, that I so much admire; sometimes, indeed, needing indulgence to eastern hyperbolism. My eulogies, too, may be founded on a postulate which all may not be ready to grant. Among the sayings and discourses imputed to him by his biographers, I find many passages of fine imagination, correct morality, and of the most lovely benevolence; and others, again, of so much ignorance, so much absurdity, so much untruth, charlatanism and imposture, as to pronounce it impossible that such contradictions should have proceeded from the same being. I separate, therefore, the gold from the dross; restore to him the former and leave the latter to the stupidity of some, and roguery of others of his disciples. Of this band of dupes and impostors, Paul was the great Coryphaeus, and first corruptor of the doctrines of Jesus." *Ibid.,* pp. 120-21.

5. *Ibid.,* p. 110.

of Justice Douglas. The root of the First Amendment in the outlook of Roger Williams appeared in Justice Douglas's decision in 1952 in *Zorach v. Clauson,* the case in which released time for religious instruction off school limits was upheld. He wrote: "We are a religious people whose institutions presuppose a Supreme Being. We guarantee the freedom to worship as one chooses. We make room for a wide variety of beliefs and creeds as the spiritual needs of man deem necessary. We sponsor an attitude on the part of the government that shows no partiality to any one group and that lets each flourish according to the zeal of its adherents and the appeal of its dogma. When the state encourages religious instruction or cooperates with religious authorities by adjusting the schedule of public events to sectarian needs, it follows the best of our traditions. For it then respects the religious nature of our people and accomodates the public service to their spiritual needs. To hold that it may not would be to find in the Constitution a requirement that the government show a callous indifference to religious groups. That would be preferring those who believe in no religion over those who do believe."

Even in this expression, the most positive recent dictum by the Supreme Court on the place of religion in American culture, there is an attenuation of the original impulse from radical Protestantism. It is not Christianity but "religion" which is for Justice Douglas the commonly accepted truth of our culture, making maximum room for other faiths and views. This notion owes something to Deism. The very name applied to God, "Supreme Being," is a term typical of the Enlightenment.

This counterimpulse is now dominant in Douglas's outlook. In the recent case of *Engel* v. *Vitale* he concurred with the decision of the court disallowing a nondenominational prayer, composed by the New York Board of Regents for use in the schools of that state. A decade after his decision in the *Zorach* case, Douglas now quotes with disapproval, as contrary to the First Amendment, the very evidence he once gave that our institutions presuppose a Supreme Being: for example, that there are chaplains paid by the government for both the House and Senate and in all the branches of the Armed Forces, that "In God We Trust" is the motto on American coinage, and so forth. Mr. Douglas has now repented of being with the majority in the *Everson* case. In the name of the First Amendment he would have every vestige of religion removed from public support: "The First Amendment leaves the Government in a position not of hostility to religion but of neutrality. The philosophy is that the atheist or agnostic—the nonbeliever —is entitled to go his own way. The philosophy is that if government interferes in matters spiritual, it will be a divisive force."

The meaning of freedom of religion for all is easy to define in a democratic state with an established church, like contemporary England. In a secularist state, like the Third French Republic, the opposing forces could be described and predicted with almost geometrical precision. In America, however, the relations between church and state are not nearly as clear-cut, because of the conflicting origins of the First Amendment. An undoctrinaire lay state was here created on the frontiers of civilization by an overwhelmingly Protestant and Christian population which, quite apart from all theories, was forced to live with an existing multiplicity of sects. It has therefore often been said that these origins, and the continuing nature of American experience as a whole, lend themselves to inevitable tensions and to *ad hoc* solutions of individual questions, that is, to constant redefinition of the boundaries between church and state. That this is what has been happening throughout our history is certainly true, and it is equally likely that it will continue to happen.

Nonetheless this is only half the story. Most of the quarrels about the First Amendment, especially the contemporary ones, have swirled around the question of how much, if any, material or moral support the state may offer religion, or the religions, in America. On this large issue there is, to say the least, neither a present concensus nor a sure guide in the American past, including the origins of the First Amendment. It is, after all, true that James Madison himself served on the committee of the First Congress which created the office of chaplain to the House and Senate. But what of the reverse question: what does the unique American experiment demand of religion, and of the religions?

This question has not been asked often enough, or clearly enough, especially in recent years. "Faith" has become too untouchable a word for it to be fashionable to raise such an issue, since it is assumed that absolute freedom of religion exists in America as nowhere else in the world. It is indeed true that our higher courts have been more zealous in their defense of this freedom than of any other constitutional guarantee. Yet there is a sense, crucial to the understanding of the American vision, in which the free society has made one essential demand on religion. Implicit in the First Amendment, in what went before it and what has flowed from it, is a "compact" between society and the religions. Society promised not to coerce the sects through the state, guaranteeing the "free exercise" of all spiritual faiths—but it is equally true that the sects were expected to pay a price for this freedom: they would no longer be permitted to coerce society.

On this point the lesson of American history is as clear as a human record can be, and all the various tones to be heard in the First Amendment are univocal. It is a closed issue, decided long ago by the Supreme Court, that the Mormons may not practice polygamy, despite a serious religious conviction commanding them to do so. A man's proving that he objects on religious grounds to bearing arms does not definitely exempt him as a matter of undeniable right from the military draft; such exemptions are only elective acts of legislative grace. It is not only in detail, however, and as it affects unpopular minority faiths that American society asserts the right to make the religions modify their practices. There is a more fundamental proposition, on which disciples of both Roger Williams and Voltaire would agree. It is this: the various sects may each continue to believe that each is the absolute vessel of God's true revelation of Himself. They are to be protected most solicitously in every right that is necessary to their exercise of persuasion on the broadest scale, and, it is self-evident, that within the private confines of each denomination it may deal in absolutist terms with those who freely elect to accept its discipline. Each of them must, however, renounce any action affecting others which it would have a right to only if its truth were absolute, that is, valid for the nonbeliever, even though he does not yet know it, or very likely may never acknowledge it. In sum, the American experiment asked, and continues to ask, something previously unknown and almost unthinkable of the religions: that they become split personalities. Each sect is to remain the one true and revealed faith for itself and in private, but each must behave in the public arena as if its truth were as tentative as an aesthetic opinion or a scientific theory.

In Western history the concept of the limited state was no new invention. Medieval political theorists had declared the state to be subordinate to natural law and the authority of the church. In the name of these ideas a pope had once made an emperor kneel in penitence in the snows of Canossa. To be sure, the limits put on a medieval monarch by the authority incarnate in the church militant are different from those assigned by a sovereign people to the new American state. Nonetheless, set though it then was in a radically different matrix, the notion of a limited state had antecedents in the Western tradition. What was really new—and unique—in the American experiment was the concept of the limited church.

Five propositions need to be stated here about this idea: it could not have developed out of theology; there is a body of American doctrine and experience, a direction to our civil polity, which is apart from the faiths and with which they have come to terms; the religions of America are sufficiently transformed by their own acceptance of the ground rules of American freedom that they can, and have, described themselves as new mutants of their various ancient faiths; this new self-definition is a more radical demand than that posed to a religion either by its establishment or by a clear threat from a state in the hands of any counterfaith, either religious or secular; and, last, the line of self-limitation is difficult to draw and it is often breached.

The concept of the limited church was a construction of history, not of theology. It arose at a moment in time when the real situation in the nascent nation, along with bits and pieces from several worlds of thought, created a certain parallelogram of forces. It was foreshadowed in the theories of Roger Williams, which became, as we have seen, a component of the American outlook, but he had not convinced the rest of American Protestantism that Calvin in Geneva, the Mathers in Massachusetts, and the Episcopalian establishment in Virginia had been wrong because they had erred in their understanding of the meaning of Christianity. The truth is fairly stated in a recent major study document produced for heirs of Calvinism in the United States, the United Presbyterian Church: "Although colonial and subsequent Presbyterians played active and dramatic roles in the evolution of the concept of church-state separation, it is a mistake to assume that this concept has grown out of any doctrine of Christian theology. Separation of church and state in the United States was not a product of theological reflection alone. In a real sense it was a decisively secular development and obtained most of its meaning from the national experience of the United States of America."[6]

6. *Relations Between Church and State*, a Report to the 174th General Assembly of the United Presbyterian Church in the United States of America, May, 1962. This point is emphasized several times in this paper. "Many Presbyterians erroneously assume that the separation of church and state is a fundamentally Protestant and primarily Presbyterian idea. This is a specifically American concept and has decisively secular origins. It does not have a churchly or theological origin. Without question, American

Among the Catholics, Father John Courtney Murray has labored hard in recent years not only to defend the First Amendment on theological grounds but almost to lay claim to it. Father Murray would deny that this arrangement contains an ideology of its own: "We have to abandon the poetry of those who would make a religion out of freedom of religion and a dogma out of separation of church and state. We have to talk prose, the prose of the Constitution itself, which is an ordinary legal prose having nothing to do with doctrinaire theories."[7] He therefore insists that the first two amendments to the Constitution represent "not articles of faith but articles of peace." The American Catholic can therefore, according to Father Murray, in good conscience live with and within the American state, which has no ideology of its own, whereas French Catholics had no choice but to fight the Jacobins in the French Revolution and the aggressively lay state of the Third Republic. Theologically Murray is enabled to accept the First Amendment by referring to the rights that the Catholic position allows to error. He quotes Pope Pius XII: "The duty of repressing religious and moral error cannot therefore be an ultimate norm of action. It must be subordinated to higher and more general norms which in *some circumstances* permit, and even perhaps make it appear the better course of action, that error should not be impeded in order to promote a greater good."[8]

Whether Father Murray's account of both American and Catholic history is correct need not greatly concern us at this point. It is simply true, as a matter of historic fact, that no

churches of the colonial period accepted the development of church-state separation for theological as well as practical reasons. Theological motivation accounts to a large extent for their active and noble involvement in the whole process. . . . But one can hardly maintain that theological reflection alone either would or could have generated what came to pass in the formative phases of the development of the American republic." *Ibid.*, p. 30.
7. John Courtney Murray, *We Hold These Truths* (New York: Sheed & Ward, 1960), p. 56.
8. *Ibid.*, pp. 61-62.

society in which the Catholic church has dominated has ever, out of Catholic theological concern for the rights of error, created civil equality for other faiths. When this has happened, it has always been forced on a formally Catholic polity by those inimical to or at least outside of that church. What appears in the very careful language of the Pope is the proposition that some countries are different from others, and the role of Catholics within them, even on so vital a matter as repressing error, must be prudently reoriented. The Catholic church in America is neither the church in Spain nor the silent church in Russia; in this view the church in America is a third and equally valid variant, within its own unique existential situation. For the American Catholic this is what, in Father Murray's words, the First Amendment means: "It does not say that there is no distinction between true and false religion, good and bad morality. But it does say that *in American circumstances* the conscience of the community, aware of its moral obligations to the peace of the community, and speaking therefore as the voice of God, does not give government any mandate, does not impose upon it any duty, and does not even communicate to it the right to repress religious opinions or practices, even though they are erroneous and false."[9] This statement is an eloquent acceptance of the situation imposed here by the American notion of the limited church; it certainly lays no claim that the Catholic tradition is its author.

There is no need to quibble over the next point, whether there is a positive body of American doctrine and outlook which has shaped the religions in this country. Protestant analysts have almost uniformly affirmed its existence while Catholics, as we have seen in the work of John Courtney Murray, tend to deny it. There is one element of truth in these Catholic views, namely, that the First Amendment was no victory for militant, doctrinaire antireligion, but the rest is mostly a question of semantics or it is self-contradictory.

9. *Ibid.*, p. 63.

Individualism and free choice in religion are typically American values. So for that matter is the notion, much invoked by Catholic spokesmen, that American society is for religion, provided all sects are treated equally. This idea is a main contemporary premise for arguments in favor of tax aid for parochial schools, but it cannot be limited to that use. The doctrine of freedom for religion points also toward the right of Protestants and most Jews to practice birth control everywhere in America, and of all Protestants and all Jews to be divorced from their spouses, if they so wish, on grounds acceptable to their own spiritual outlooks. Indeed, each of the faiths best demonstrates its devotion to these principles of religious freedom and equality not when its own interests are endangered but by its attitude when the ox of another religion is being gored.

What has kept a measure of peace among the sects is the wish of the overarching American tradition that the sects limit their warfare even in the public arena of persuasion and certainly in the realms of coercion. Left to themselves, the major faiths of the Western world have not thought about each other very much, except as objects of conversion. Implicit within the American stance on freedom of religion is pressure on the various groups to presume that the others are here to stay. What terms one may wish to use for such an outlook is irrelevant. That it has shaped the religions in America by more than providing them with blank space in which to expand and collide seems undeniable. Certainly, as Catholics in particular have often pointed out, Jefferson's assertion that all men are endowed by the Creator with some inalienable rights is a positive doctrine with roots in natural law, not an unideological and neutral *tabula rasa* on which Americans can write what they like. Have not the rights to life, liberty, and the pursuit of happiness been a different matrix for shaping the religions in America from, let us say, a doctrine about the purpose of human life as perfect obedience to a perfect law?

Protestants, even at their most conservative, are comfortable with a multiplicity of churches reflecting differing national traditions. The value of national traditions wedded to religion is the validation of establishment wherever it still exists. The assertion that their church in all its varieties is different in America therefore causes Protestants no grief. Such a thought produces a dilemma for Catholics. To allow a large difference to develop between one group of believers and the rest of the church calls its universality into question. Therefore the notion that the Roman church is different in America in any important respect must be denied, for theological reasons. On the other hand, there are practical considerations of the highest order which have made and make it necessary for precisely this to be affirmed with vigor and even vehemence. In the bitter debate about the Catholic faith which marked the political campaign of 1960, Catholics in America were charged with everything that had ever happened in the Middle Ages or was happening in places like contemporary Spain. Their essential answer was to insist that America was different and that they had been made different by assenting to the American experiment and by living loyally within it. This is true. It is inconceivable today in America that Roman Catholic priests should be involved in the leadership of an anti-Semitic movement, though this is precisely what is happening in Argentina, where the hierarchy has not silenced priests who are spokesmen for the racist Tacuara organization.[10] Whether these differences are to be defined as matters of detail or essence can be left to those most immediately concerned. To the analyst from the outside it appears that in actual fact something crucial happened in the 1960 election beyond the fact that a Catholic was elected President. At the height of that campaign several important statements were made on

10. *New York Times,* Sept. 12. 1962. See also the *Daily Bulletin* of the Jewish Telegraphic Agency for Oct. 3, 1962. Father Carlos Cuechetti, the cofounder of the Argentine Jewish-Christian Fraternity, is quoted there as follows: "We cannot affirm that the Church hierarchically organizes and incites anti-Semitism but it can be said that the hierarchy has not adopted steps to prevent such outbursts generated in Catholic institutions and schools."

behalf of the American hierarchy. They amounted to a formal promise to abide by the self-limiting tradition of the sects in America, that is, to behave in actual practice as one among many churches. Thus the inevitable price was "paid" for full entry into American society.[11]

We must conclude this point with one further observation. American freedom has more fundamentally altered the religions than either of the more usual alternatives: establishment of religion or battle with an aggressively lay or ideologically hostile state. An absolutist faith most certainly maintains its outlook when established, even if it makes a few concessions for error. Minority faiths can look at an established church with the self-righteous anger of those in Babylonian captivity. As against a lay state, or even a communist one, the church or churches sent into the wilderness can continue to be certain of their respective absolute truths. What the church wanted of the Third Republic, was not, after all, equal freedom for all religions, but the restoration, at very least, of some part of its role in the schools. What it wants today in communist Poland is not cultural neutrality but the restoration of its influence in public life.

Having made a unique "social compact" with society, it is no secret that the churches in America have not always lived up to the self-denying ordinance that was involved. There has indeed been some bad faith by the various sects, as they have consciously reneged on the promise by trying to enact into laws for all views which they knew were parochial to themselves. Annoying though this is, it is really the less important aspect of the problem. More fundamentally the sects have often sincerely believed that their views were coextensive with the civil consensus of America. Prohibition, for instance, descended from Puritanism but it was voted in as a civil decision—and to my knowledge no one has sued recently in the states with local option on the ground that such a law was an invasion of his religious freedom by his being made

11. *New York Times*, Sept. 28, 1960 and Oct. 28, 1960.

137

to conform to someone else's religious concepts. Last year the blue law cases were lost in the Supreme Court. Chief Justice Warren admitted the origin of these regulations in Christianity but he accepted the argument that they were now purely civil arrangements.[12]

The religions in America do not, however, merely differ as to what belongs in the American cultural and social consensus to which they have assented. Each sect asks itself, and is challenged by others, as to how much did it concede, irretrievably, in accepting the American pluralism. Inevitably this involves the individual denominations in a further question: what can each afford to concede, and what is so essential to its faith, survival, or self-respect that under present conditions it must be fought for without compromise? Jewish opinion, for example, does not regard the blue law issue as closed by

12. "If the purpose or effect of a law is to impede the observance of one or all religions or is to discriminate invidiously between religions that law is constitutionally invalid even though the burden may be characterized as being only indirect. But if the State regulates conduct by enacting a general law within its power, the purposes and effect of which is to advance the State's secular goals, the statute is valid despite its indirect burden on religious observance unless the State may accomplish its purpose by means which do not impose such a burden." (Chief Justice Earl Warren in re *Braunfeld* v. *Brown*, Supreme Court, May 29, 1961.)

I do not mean to imply that Warren's views represent any desire to enact Christianity. The meaning of his decision is made clearer in Justice Frankfurter's concurring view, which proposes the notion that if something can fairly be called part of our American civil consensus, regardless of its origin, this rule may then indirectly coerce one or the other of the sects. Justice Douglas, in dissent, denied this, root and branch, insisting, as he was later to say in *Engel* v. *Vitale*, that absolute separation of church and state must be enforced. Justices Brennan and Stewart implied that the Sunday laws were indeed part of the American consensus, but that the First Amendment made it incumbent on the state to make life as easy for Sabbatarians as for the majority: "In fine, the Court, in my view, has exalted administrative convenience to a constitutional level high enough to justify this result on the ground that the effect on religion, though substantial, is indirect. The Court forgets, I think, a warning uttered during the congressional discussion of the First Amendment itself: '. . . the rights of conscience are, in their nature, of peculiar delicacy, and will little bear the gentlest touch of governmental hand. . . .'" What this amounts to, it seems to me, is the assertion that social peace in America is a bargain between society and its subgroups, and especially with and among its religions, with a presumption in favor of minority religious conscience even against the "administrative convenience" of society.

Justice Warren's decision blanketing these ordinances into our American secular order. Catholics are not entirely of one mind as to whether the legal precedents do or do not admit of tax support for parochial schools, but they are almost unanimous in believing that such aid must be forthcoming. If there is a past consensus against such action, they insist that it is time for a change in outlook.

Be it noted that certain glittering abstractions are being used by all the parties to these arguments, but none of these theories are really the dogma of those who profess them. The Catholic argument on parochial schools is usually grounded in the principles of distributive justice and equal freedom for all religions. These ideas have served to make an effective case on this issue; it has not propelled the major weight of Catholic influence to fight beside Jews against the blue laws, so that Sabbatarians, too, might enjoy distributive justice and religious equality. On the contrary, the most effective organized opposition to any new legislative exceptions has come from some Catholic quarters. Comparably, on the very matter of tax aid for parochial schools Protestants for the most part keep insisting on the "wall of separation" between church and state. However, the conservative Protestants who are most vehement on this point tend to be equally vehement against those Jews who invoke the principle of separation in order to exclude Christmas from the public schools. Official Jewish policy on the generality of church-state questions, for that matter, has overwhelmingly been based on a quite doctrinaire interpretation of the First Amendment, but this has not led the Jewish community to press for the lifting of tax exemptions from all religious institutions, including its own.

It is clear that many of the arguments being used in the current great debate can be demolished in the name of consistency. They are much less important than the real issues: the needs and fears of the various components of our religiously plural society. This age is too conscious of history to content itself with abstract argument, either one's own or that of others, and not to ask the question: why does he think that way? What set of prior experiences does his thinking reflect? We are too taken with the concreteness of this moment in time to believe that we can deal with someone else unless we can appreciate his world as he sees it. Therefore what the communions should put on view is not their most effective debaters' points but a description of the religious situation, their own and others, as it appears to them in all its concreteness. This will no doubt wound. It also runs counter to the palpable but much cherished myth that "the others" do not really know the innermost problems, or the closed-door talk, of the respective in-groups. But such self-portraits, "warts and all," are more likely to affect others than all the formal paraphernalia of persuasion.

# II

Our contemporary Western culture as a whole, and American culture in particular, has often been called post-Christian. The first word in that hyphenated term is generally the one that is emphasized, to point the distance we have gone from the age of faith. There is, however, a vantage point from which the continuing Christian mode of our culture is the more evident. The whole of the civil calendar of the West is Christian and our culture remains the culture of Christendom, if not of Christianity. The contemporary Christmas is indeed all too pagan, but it is a Christian paganism—certainly not a Jewish or Moslem one. I insisted above that a self-limiting premise, to distinguish between faith in one's own absolute and a relativism in making claims on society, was part of the "bargain" that launched American religious pluralism. This sundering between private faith and public policy is most clear in Judaism, for the inherent bargains which marked the entry of this faith into the modern West were not masked. The society with which Judaism dealt was not continuing in a secularized way some of its religious traditions.

Here the process was not ambiguous—but the example of this clarity has also often been annoying to the Christian faiths, for they are sometimes more comfortable with the ambiguities.

Many Americans would like to assume that a lowest-common-denominator Christianity compounded out of non-denominational prayers of Christian origin, the Christmas spirit, especially in the public schools, and other comparable forms of public piety is self-evident and unquestionable in American life. It is by now forgotten that Catholics once fought bitterly against this very construction, in order to protect their children in the public schools from indoctrination in this sub-Protestant religion, and that they were then the protagonists of the most doctrinaire reading of the First Amendment. In the 1840's there were furious battles over Bible reading in the public schools, a practice which Catholics then opposed because the version in use was Protestant, and, more generally, because they maintained that to read the Bible without emphasizing the sole interpreting authority of the church was to lead Catholics astray. In New York the results of the argument were inconclusive; in Philadelphia there was a riot in 1844, in which thirteen people were killed. An investigating grand jury then blamed the event on the Catholics: had they not spearheaded "the efforts of a portion of the community to exclude the Bible from our Public Schools."[13] There were battles of comparable nature, though fortunately less bloody, throughout the nineteenth century and even the first several decades of the twentieth. As recently as 1951 a Roman Catholic and a Jew jointly sued the Board of Education of Rutherford, New Jersey, to prevent the distribution of Gideon Bibles in the schools, on the ground that they are sectarian books.

This phase in the experience of Catholics in America is now ancient history. In the outbursts that followed after the decision in June, 1962, forbidding the Regents' Prayer in New

13. Ray Allen Billington, *The Protestant Crusade, 1800-1860: A Study of the Origins of American Nativism* (New York: Rinehart, 1938), pp. 222-231.

York State, some Catholics took the lead in condemning the outcome and in deploring Jewish participation in the suit against the practice. Public school religion was summarily included in the content of the continuing American consensus by these spokesmen, notably by the editors of the Jesuit weekly, *America,* and Jews were asked: "What will have been accomplished if our Jewish friends win all the legal immunities they seek, but thereby paint themselves into a corner of social and cultural alienation?"[14] It does not really advance the present discussion to point out, in further detail, how inconsistent this statement is with past Catholic positions. Nor will it really help if one proves, as it is easy to do, that having accepted an essentially Protestant view of the function of religion and of public education, this leaves Catholics on far weaker ground in arguing against Protestants for their own parochial schools. The testiness displayed by *America* has roots in a popular mood in which the mass of Protestants and Catholics are united. A Gallup poll taken in August, 1962, after the Supreme Court decision in *Engel* v. *Vitale* (the Regents' Prayer case), showed that four out of five American Christians, regardless of denomination, favor religious exercises in the public schools. There is no appreciable change in view among men and women of higher educational level and the only sectional difference is that the proportion is even higher in the South, despite the well known devotion of the Southern Baptist leadership to the principle of separation. Only the Jews dissent, for only one in five sees merit in any form of religious expression (presumably even of the Hanukkah-Christmas variety) in the schools.

These existential facts mean at least this: the mass of Christians in America are for something which the majority of Jews oppose. Catholics and Protestants appear willing to strike a bargain on the basis of favoring a Christian-flavored patriotism as the not so tacitly formalized religion of America; in the interest of such an arrangement many are willing to

14. *America,* Sept. 1, 1962.

bend or ignore the First Amendment. Most Protestants and Catholics see no affront to the palpable interests of their faiths from such a consensus—though as we shall see later, there are vital differences of mood, intent, and intensity of feeling between the two groups.

Jews can defend themselves against such pressure in three possible ways. The first is to point out to the Christian majority that this particular version of the consensus can, conceivably, be used against Christianity. If society, for example, can enact blue laws for Sunday for Chief Justice Warren's reasons, a legislature composed of Seventh Day Adventists and Jews might, as Justice Douglas has suggested, proceed to discommode Christians by voting in blue laws for Saturday. In the second place, Jews can and do argue that the self-limiting bargain struck by the sects means, at very least, that the believers of each will be treated with tender consideration by all the rest and that, for instance, to impose Christmas on Jewish children in the schools is as wrong as would be attempts to make much of Passover in the public school of a largely Jewish neighborhood. The practical trouble with both these approaches is that they are shared by many reflective Christians, who have arrived at such conclusions quite independently, but they are rejected by the mass, to whom a Jewish-dominated legislature enacting Saturday blue laws or a public school system invaded by Passover is not a real and present danger. For most of them "atheistic communism," in the much used phrase, is. They suggest that the defense against Khrushchev, juvenile delinquency, and many other threats, foreign and domestic, is to be found in an increased public piety. What if Jewish children sing Christmas carols in the public school, some ask, or are taught to recite the Lord's Prayer? Isn't this but a small price for a minority to pay when the future of the world is at stake? The remaining defense available to Jews, at very least as a tactic and tool, has been to try to shelter behind the "wall of separation," in its most doctrinaire interpretation.

It would, however, be an error to "forgive" the Jews for being on the same side, here, with atheists, secularists, and the like simply because they cannot help themselves, tactically. Although there are deep differences of outlook within the Jewish community, it is nonetheless correct to assert that the weight of contemporary Jewish feeling and opinion—and not for mere tactical reasons—supports the view that there ought to be the strictest kind of separation between church and state and even between the church and society. In all truth, among some this passion for a secular public society has indeed been a reflection, in part, of their alienation from their own religious and historic roots, but this is really a minor part of the story. Its essence is in the fact that what the Jew is trying to express, in the language of constitutional law and in the context of contemporary America, is a reflection of a process with long roots in Jewish faith and history. Such words as "religion," "secularism," and "society" have meanings in the Christian tradition, and in post-Christian Western secularism, which it is presumed have the same resonance for Jews. The truth is that they do not. Jews differ from Christians not only in conclusions but, more seriously, in premises and in stance. We must therefore attempt to understand those aspects of Judaism and Jewish experience in the past which have fashioned the present outlook.

A tension between government and religion is the essence of the prophetic experience. When the tribes of Israel pressed Samuel to sanction the choice of a king, he resisted in the name of a theocratic ideal, that God Himself should be king, but Samuel failed to prevent the election of Saul. From that day forward it was never again seriously maintained that any civil power, not even the most God-fearing of the kings, could claim the place of Moses, who united within himself the roles of king, priest, and prophet. The royal power was under constant criticism. Though David, for example, was on generally good terms with the prophets, Nathan boldly confronted him with his sin in the affair of Bathsheba (II

Samuel 13:12). What is implicit in this story, and in Elijah's later denouncing of Ahab after he had stolen the vineyard of Naboth, is a central theme of the Bible. Kings and magistrates are not absolute; the king is certainly not, as elsewhere in the Near East of that day, a divine being, the son of God; the state itself is limited by divine law.

There was, of course, no concept of separation of church and state in ancient Israel. The Holy Temple in Jerusalem was erected in the time of Solomon not by private subscription but by the maximum effort of a king who did not hesitate to tax heavily for this purpose. Formal religion was so closely interwoven with the state in the days of the biblical kings that perhaps the most crucial action in the revolt of Jeroboam, which divided the ten northern tribes into the separate kingdom of Israel, was his establishment of a competing temple in Bethel. He thus cemented his kingdom by giving it a center for its own state religion, and he further detached the northern tribes from the attraction of the religiopolitical authority in Jerusalem (I Kings, 12:26-33). It is this very religion of kings and priests, however, which is the constant target of prophetic anger. The office of speaking the divine truth to power was not easy, and each of the prophets tried to avoid the danger by resisting God's call to him. Their lives were indeed stormy and dangerous, but it is noteworthy that the very kings who were being bitterly denounced never put a prophet to death. This cannot be explained as merely accidental; there was a clear presumption even on the part of wicked kings that prophecy was a valid religious office. The denunciations were not heeded, but neither were they really suppressed.

I do not suggest that prophetic criticism of kings and society was in the name of the principle of freedom of religious thought. Elijah's chief purpose against Ahab was not to assert the right for himself to think and worship as he pleased. On the contrary, he was fighting against a kind of religious pluralism in which the Jewish God was being worshiped in Israel along with Baal and the rest of the pantheon that Jezebel had brought with her. The man who stood on Mount Carmel alone beside his altar, confronting the priests of Baal surrounding theirs, was no contemporary liberal divine. He was there in the service of the jealous God who had commanded, in the Decalogue: "Thou shalt have no other gods before me." In His name Elijah cried out to an unanswering people, "how long will you halt between two opinions; if God is the Lord, follow Him; if Baal, follow him" (I Kings 18:21). The prophets did not arise to separate religion from the state but to replace false religion with divine truth. But they failed over and over again, and even their successes endured but for a moment. Prophecy could never abandon its critical function, which continued throughout the whole of the biblical age. The result was to establish the presumptions that no state could be trusted without reservation, that the official religion of the state was likely to be an empty form, and that true religion was likely to mean standing apart, and probably even standing over against, the state.

The biblical source of contemporary Jewish attitudes on church and state is, however, to be found only to a secondary degree in the obvious place to look, in the relationship of king and religion in ancient Israel. Their true root is in another aspect of the prophetic mission, in that overarching vision of the Messiah which is the unifying theme of biblical prophecy. Prophetic attention was not merely turned inward, to the evils within Jewish society. The great days of prophecy coincided with several centuries of constant threat and danger to both the Jewish kingdoms. Palestine was situated at the crossroads of the great and warring empires of Egypt, Assyria, and, later, Babylonia. As the northern kingdom fell and the shadows kept deepening for the one in the south, prophetic chastisement alternated with more hopeful visions of redemption. The messianic dream became all the more necessary and all the more poignant and ecstatic when the exiles wept by the waters of Babylon. Let these verses speak for this greatest of all the prophetic themes:

> "And it shall come to pass in the end of days
> That the mountain of the Lord's house
> Shall be established as the top of the mountains,
> And it shall be exalted above the hills,
> And all nations shall flow unto it.
> And many people shall go, and say:
> 'Come, let us go up to the mountain of the Lord,
> To the house of the God of Jacob,
> And he will teach us His ways,
> And we will walk in His paths.'
> For the law shall come forth from Zion,
> And the word of the Lord from Jerusalem.
> And He shall judge the nations,
> And shall decide for many peoples;
> And they shall beat their swords into ploughshares
> And their spears into pruning-hooks.
> Nation shall not lift up sword against nation,
> Neither shall they learn war anymore."
>
> (Isaiah II: 2-4)

The Return under the leadership of Nehemiah and Ezra did result in the rebuilding of the Temple and the establishment of Jewish self-government, but this was no "end of days." Empires continued to clash and the people of the Lord was evermore a small sheep among the wolves. Amidst these dangers, and especially during the travail of the battles of the Maccabees with the Syrian Greeks and their Jewish collaborators, the prophetic themes recurred, in the Apocrypha and in the vision of the end of days in the book of Daniel: the Lord will surely save his people and vindicate it against its enemies; He will make an end of the last wicked empire so that peace might reign. Such hope became all the more necessary after the destruction of the Second Temple in the year 70. It soon became clear that succor would be long in coming, for repeated revolts in the first few decades after that event failed and no miraculous deliverance intervened. As the

Exile wore on, with all the tragic horrors of expulsions, pogroms, and persecutions with which most of centuries since its beginning have been laden, Jews were sustained in their travail and their waiting by the Messianic vision. That hope is reaffirmed in the prayer with which every Jewish service, without exception, is always concluded: "We therefore hope in thee, O Lord our God, that we may speedily behold the glory of thy might, when thou wilt remove the abominations from the earth, and the idols will be utterly cut off, when the world will be perfected under the kingdom of the Almighty, and all the children of flesh will call upon thy name, when thou wilt turn unto thyself all the wicked of the earth. Let all the inhabitants of the world perceive and know that unto thee every knee must bow, every tongue must swear. Before thee, O Lord our God, let them bow and fall; and unto thy glorious name let them give honour; let them all accept the yoke of thy kingdom, and do thou reign over them speedily, and forever and ever. For the kingdom is thine, and to all eternity thou wilt reign in glory; as it is written in thy Law, the Lord shall reign for ever and ever. And it is said, And the Lord shall be king over all the earth: in that day shall the Lord be One, and his name One."

The classic Jewish Messianic vision, which has been expounded here at some length, may seem remote from the very tangible issues involved in church and state, but it is not. In the nineteenth century many of the religious ideals of the Western tradition were translated into this-worldly terms. So, Christianity was redefined in the "social gospel" as a movement for reform in the here and now, and in the same way Jews were to imagine that their messianic hopes could be achieved in this world. In such reinterpretation the old dreams became the central content of Jewish modernity and, as we shall see, a keystone of the Jewish attitude on church and state.

Throughout the Bible, including the prophets, the Jews are most emphatically a special treasure of God's but the counter-theme of His equal concern for all the nations and all the peoples is constantly reaffirmed. "Behold, you children of Israel are to Me like the Ethiopians, saith the Lord: I brought Israel out of Egypt and the Philistines from Caphtor and Aram from Kir" (Amos 9:7). Such thinking produced the classic rabbinic view about non-Jews that is expressed in both doctrine and law. The doctrine is that salvation is not a monopoly of the Jews: "The righteous of all peoples have a share in the world to come."[15] In law, the most ancient authorities defined the rule of "the seven commandments given to the children of Noah." This basic law, which applied to all men, prohibited idolatry, adultery, bloodshed, profaning God's name, robbery, cutting flesh or a limb from a living animal, and injustice.[16] Two implications of this "law of nations" need to be noted, for our present purpose. Except for the prohibition of idolatry,[17] all the rest of these commandments are concerned with overt action, not subjective doctrine. It has always been the Jewish attitude, even in regard to the conduct of Jews and *a fortiori* with respect to all other men, that motivations and dogmas are far less than important than conduct. It is presumed that men of other faiths will indeed have faith, especially in divine judgment over their actions,[18] but the emphasis is on the moral nature of what men do. The place where all men meet is the realm of deeds. This is subject to moral judgment, and it must be guided among all men by moral principles. Even in the most orthodox of ancient Jewish views the area to be controlled by this "natural law" is severely limited, and motives and dogmas are left almost entirely to the private concern of individuals.

This emphasis on deed, as against creed, is so strongly ingrained in Judaism that Jews, who are of course required to believe as well as to do, are addressed by God, in an ancient rabbinic hyperbole, as follows: "Would that they would for-

15. *Tosefta* 13:2.
16. Babylonian Talmud, *Sanhedrin* 56a.
17. Even in the matter of idolatry, the law is mitigated: only overt worship of idols is prohibited and not faith in them (*Sanhedrin* 56b).
18. Maimonides, *Yad, Hilkhot Melakhim 4.*

America Is Different

sake me, provided that they observed My Law."[19] One result that flows naturally from such an attitude is that "faith" simply does not mean for the Jew what it is presumed to mean in the Western, that is, Greco-Christian, tradition. To assent to the right principles and to experience prayer as the essence of spiritual cultivation—these are important to Judaism but they are not the central cast of this religion. The Jew is predisposed to worship God by following an objective code of conduct, all the while pondering the spiritual principles implicit in the rule. He will ask questions of the conduct but not of the faith of men of other persuasions.

Seemingly endless centuries of exile evoked not only dreams of redemption. The very fact that the Jews were living permanently, until "the end" should come, under alien political power raised two questions: Was such power legitimate at all? If it was, what are the limits of its authority? This problem had first been faced by Jeremiah, in the very beginning of the first Exile. He sent a message from Jerusalem to Babylon, prophesying that the return was not imminent. He therefore advised the exiles in God's name to live normal lives, "and seek you the peace of the city to which I have exiled you, and pray for it to God, for in its peace will you have peace" (Jeremiah 29:7).

In this spirit the principle of "the seven commandments given to the children of Noah" was searched for the source of authority of civil governments. Rabbinic jurists in the Talmud held that the prohibition against injustice meant that governments were empowered to establish law courts. By extension, it was ruled that civil government as a whole was lawful and to be obeyed. This principle was under some question in the early days of Roman oppression, as revolts kept smoldering after the destruction of the Second Temple. The rabbis of the Talmud continued to assert, then and later, that any gentile power ruling over the Holy Land was illegitimate *de jure*. Nonetheless it was declared sinful not to pay taxes, even in

19. Palestinian Talmud, *Hagigah* 1:7.

150

Occupied Palestine. Certainly there was never doubt in the law of the Talmud that civil governments everywhere else were legitimate. This law was limited by two provisos: some rabbis held that discriminatory taxes, or other civil ordinances that were designed to oppress Jews in particular, could be evaded, though other rabbis denied even this; secondly, beyond a shadow of a doubt, any civil ordinance that commands the breaking of a law of God must be resisted, even to the limit of martyrdom.[20]

This rapid journey through some aspects of biblical and rabbinic thought has indicated certain predispositions of the Jewish faith. To summarize, the prophetic faith may have aspired to be established over all Israel, but it had to spend its entire career fighting the powers that be. The Messianic vision involved Jews in the dream of an age when all peoples and traditions would realize that they were equal in the sight of God. Millennia of experience as a small people amid great empires and, worse, as an exiled minority evoked doctrines of a moral law of conduct common to all men and of the legitimacy of governments which left men free to pursue their own religious convictions.

One does not have to be a profound student of Bible and Talmud to be able to marshal citations against this entire construction. To quote just one piece of evidence, the liberal attitude about other faiths described above is controverted by the well known fact that Judaism was a conversionist religion on a very large scale in Roman times. Indeed, the audiences which heard Paul on his missionary journeys were heavily studded with recent converts, or half-converts, to Judaism. For that matter, the objectivity of the standard proposed by Judaism to all men, that is, the moral law, is not really objective at all, but a summary of biblical morality. Like any form of

20. The two most recent authoritative discussions of the law of the Talmud on the authority of government are in Hebrew: *Talmudic Encyclopedia* (Jerusalem, 1956), Vol. VII, cols. 295-308; Gedalyahu Alon, *The History of the Jews in Palestine in the Period of the Mishneh and Talmud* (Tel Aviv, 1952), Vol. I, pp. 335-342.

natural law, it is a projection of certain major values of the faith that proposed these rules. Such objections, whether historical or philosophical, are, however, irrelevant. I am not asserting that the principles detailed above represent the Jewish dogmas in this area; they are rather one of several possible ways of Jewish feeling and thinking. That this mode has become dominant, especially in modern times, is not attributable to its logical consistency. No religion is untouched by history; it is more nearly true of Judaism than of any other faith that it has been fashioned by what has happened to it. These themes from the Bible and Talmud are important, in this configuration, because they, rather than other values also potentially present in the tradition, have been evoked and underscored by Jewish experience in the Western world.

Historians have generally emphasized that the Jewish community prior to its political emancipation (which is nowhere more than two centuries old) was dominated by its own "established" faith. Was not Spinoza excommunicated for heresy by the rabbis of Amsterdam? Indeed he was, but unlike Christian heretics without number he was not burned at the stake. To be sure, the ghetto commmunity was monolithic and highly disciplined, but its pressures could operate only on people who chose afresh every day to resist apostasy. The only kind of apostasy that was ever a crime against the state in Christian Europe was defection from the dominant faith. On the other hand, it was not a crime but a virtue, in the eyes of the wielders of political power, for a Jew to leave Judaism and become a Christian. He who did escaped the burdens of persecution and was often treated with special consideration. The Jews were, therefore, not merely under persistent pressure and temptation throughout the Middle Ages to defect from their faith; they were the sole community in the Christian West in such a situation. What greater proof did the Jews need that religion could be sustained without the prop of the power of the state?

The persisting experience of the Jew with the state in medieval Europe was to cower before its enmity. He could only hope, in the words of the oft-repeated prayer, that "the hearts of kings and princes be turned with favor towards Thy people Israel." The state was more likely to be neutral or somewhat well disposed to Jews when its ruler was little influenced by prelates. It is true that there were occasions in European Jewish history when the church protected Jews against rapacious princes, but such events were the exception. The norm was foreshadowed at the very beginning, when Christianity was established in the Roman empire by Constantine. Almost immediately there was persecution of the Jews in the name of the true faith. A few decades later the Emperor Julian, known to history as the Apostate, attempted to disestablish the church and create equality for all religions, including paganism. This gave him a bad name for many centuries, but Jews remember that he offered them freedom and that he even wished to encourage their rebuilding of the Temple in Jerusalem. But this was the exception. More usually, as in medieval Spain, Jewish existence became ever less tolerable as the power of the church grew in the state. In Spain the final expulsion in 1492 occurred under the most religiously obedient of all the Spanish rulers, Ferdinand and Isabella. Further examples to sustain this point could be marshaled almost without number, but there is no point to repeating the endless tale of the persecution of the Jews.

All the centuries of pain add up to two points that are relevant to our present concerns. In the hard school of suffering Jews have learned to feel almost instinctively that their freedom is safest—indeed that they can even achieve freedom—only in societies in which the church is blunted in its dominance of public life. It is becoming clearer through contemporary research into modern Jewish history that one of the seeds of the emancipation of the Jews was planted in the seventeenth and eighteenth centuries by mercantilist powers, which were ceasing to think of the state as Christian and were therefore more hospitable to any people who brought realistic advantage

**153**

to the country. In the second place, Jewish experience with inimical rulers can be summarized in what the greatest of contemporary Jewish historians, Salo Baron, has called almost a "law": the Jews and Judaism are better off, and feel safer, in a society or political body which is pluralist, containing a number of national groups and religious sects, than they are in a unitary political or religious structure. Thus the other seed of modern Jewish freedom is in the agreement to end the wars of religion in Europe in the seventeenth century by establishing religious diversity as the norm of western Christendom. The multinational and multireligious Austro-Hungarian empire was a far happier place for Jews than the racist and monolithic Germany of Adolf Hitler.

Enough has now been said about both Jewish religion and Jewish history to prove beyond a shadow of doubt that the devotion of the Jews to a neutral, secular state has deep roots. It is congruent with the total Jewish past and not a modern rebellion against it. The sense of being alien to power, and separate from it, has pervaded Judaism on many levels; it is a fairly recent experience for Christianity, and all of its parts are not yet accustomed to this new turn.

Modern experience has underscored this difference. The rise of the modern secular state was the *sine qua non* to the political emancipation of the Jews. On the other hand this very process, culminating in various forms of separation of church and state, has meant in the history of Christianity its moving over to a position of lesser power in men's affairs. This decline has involved the Protestant faith as well as the Catholic, but the confrontation has been most direct in the case of the Catholic church. It is not for nothing that the liberal revolution in all its implications was condemned by Pius IX in the *Syllabus of Errors* which he promulgated in 1864. His censure of the separation of church and state, religious liberty and public education is no longer Catholic doctrine, certainly not in America. However, it is one thing to make peace with the secular state because you really cannot help yourself; it is quite another to hail it as your liberator from age-old oppressions, because the nonsecular state that was its predecessor was your enemy.

Here we have arrived at the heart of the matter: the different meanings in Jewish and Western history of anti-Semitism. The mainstream of Western thought, both Christian and post-Christian, affirms that the history of the West has been a good human record with many blotches, among them hatred of the Jew. Therefore, except for the initiators of radical revolutionary movements, few doubt that Western experience should continue in the general direction in which it has been going, with the necessary reforms to broaden and purify the culture. The end of anti-Semitism is generally included as one among the reforms to be instituted by a progressive West. Many Jews have joined and continue to join with gentiles in affirming this Reformism, at least with their heads, and in believing that it will ultimately be adequate to end their danger. Nevertheless, with the forebodings of their hearts most Jews do not believe this at all. The West has produced too many pogroms, *auto-da-fés*, and Auschwitz's for Jews to believe, with Olympian calm, that this is an unfortunate but accidental feature of European civilization and that it will go away some day. The Jews must diagnose the Western tradition as not merely prone to the virus of anti-Semitism but as endemically ill with the disease. Therefore, for their own safety and for the lives of their children, Jews must look for a radical change in the very foundations of Western civilization, so that it should not spawn future assaults on themselves.

In the light of what has just been said, the central meanings of the most important modern Jewish outlooks are to be seen in a new, paradoxical light. It has generally been assumed that Zionism is the most radical attack, based on the most pessimistic estimate of anti-Semitism, that the Jews have ever mounted against European culture. The various other movements of Jewish modernity, which represent forms of acculturation, are supposed to be more accomodating approaches to the relationship between Jew and Gentile. This is the surface truth. In essence the story is in reverse.

The heart of the Zionist position is in two propositions: that all basic identities are, or ought to be, national; and that anti-Semitism, aggravated though it is, is but the most pervasive and intense form of an essentially rational phenomenon that can really be changed with simple ease. Theodor Herzl, the founder of modern Zionism, asserted that it was the "abnormality" of the Jew, as a minority everywhere, that had aggravated the normal tensions between national groups into the peculiarly grave form of anti-Semitism. He argued that the Jew should, therefore, reorganize his identity into the normal Western form, becoming one among the many species of the genus "nation," and all the old hatreds would automatically disappear. Zionism is consistent in granting that the Western tradition consists of various national cultures, and it has deep understanding for the fact that culture is more than political identity. Identity is also history and, even for the irreligious, it is the stamp that the religious past has laid on national culture. Zionists are, therefore, willing to admit that in some fundamental sense Western culture remains pervasively Christian. They presume that there can and ought to be, for the sake of everybody's peace and dignity, a comparable Jewish national culture. This culture can be (indeed in Israel it largely is) post-Jewish, but it will be at least as related to its own past as contemporary post-Christianity is related to the historic values and experiences of the church.

This conception of religion and culture was expressed recently in an important way in the decision by the Supreme Court of the state of Israel in the case of Brother Daniel. A Catholic monk of Jewish birth, he had been admitted to Israel and was, in its law, free to ask for naturalization as a citizen of the state. He sued for automatic admission under an act fundamental to Israel's outlook, the provision that any Jew, of any provenance, can automatically demand citizenship in Israel. Brother Daniel wished to be given an identity card under this law, and he asked to be described as a Jew by nationality and a Catholic by faith. One minority view in the Supreme Court of Israel supported this demand, in the name of the absolute separation of religion and national identity. The majority opinion was delivered by Chief Justice Silberg: "I have not come to preach religiosity and I do not represent any particular view as to a proper future development of the Jewish people. I know that opinions about what is or ought to be are widely at variance in Israel, reflecting all the colors of our broad cultural rainbow, from the most religious to the completely atheistic, but one thing is held in common by all parts of the people which dwells in Zion (except for a miniscule minority), and it is this: We are not cutting ourselves off from the historic past, and we are not denying our ancestral heritage. We are continuing to drink from the original sources. The forms are different, the conduits are different, the conclusions are different, but we are not stopping up the wells, for without them we would be the poorest of the poor. Only a fool would believe or think that we are here creating a new culture, for—it is much too late! A people which is almost as old as mankind itself does not start *ab ovo*, and our new culture in this land will be, even in the most extreme possible version, only a new edition of the past."

This view had implications beyond the borders of Israel. Even there Justice Silberg was not speaking of an identity between political status and the religioculture that pervades the state, for Brother Daniel can, and no doubt will, be naturalized as a citizen. His rights to every consideration for his faith will be guarded zealously, but within a society which is overwhelmingly and publicly Jewish. Comparably, one would have to say that Jews are, and must be, politically indistinguishable from all other citizens in, let us say, America, but that the religiocultural issues are on a different plane. The state is neutral, but the majority culture is Christian. Jews must, on the one hand, accept the notion that they are culturally in the minority; therefore some temperate expressions of the majority

157

outlook (for example, not overly Christological Christmas celebrations in the public schools) are as proper in public institutions as are Purim carnivals in the schools of Tel Aviv. What the Jews have a right to ask is that they be treated with every consideration a majority can offer the sensibilities and sensitivities of a minority. This view has indeed been maintained by many spokesmen for Orthodox Judaism, who share with Catholics the feeling that each faith ought to be a religiocultural entity, with some basic institutions of its own, including parochial schools.[21] It has appeared recently in the writings of several more liberal Jewish thinkers.[22]

The major thrust of Jewish modernity, from its beginnings in Europe, has, however, been in another, essentially *less* accomodating direction. There remained, in prayer and in pervading consciousness, the old dream of the Messianic age as the day of "a new heaven and a new earth," when all the old order of the world would be overturned completely and the woes of the Jews would disappear automatically. The most expansive Jewish spirits saw the beginnings of political emancipation at the dawn of the nineteenth century as the first step toward achieving such an age, in this world and by human agency. Was not progress the god of the age? Had not the advanced minds of the Enlightenment envisaged a world in which all "medievalism," that is, all artificial differences and oppressions among men, would disappear in the name of the oneness of humanity?

To repeat, medieval history and experience were soaked in Jewish blood. It was inevitable that, to a greater degree than any other community, the Jews would look with hope toward truly radical change. After many centuries of being excluded, the Jew wanted to become not merely a citizen but a brother. This is the source of the well known passion of many Jews for all the new ideas of the eighteenth and nineteenth centuries,

21. See, for example, Rabbi Menachem M. Schneerson, in *Commonweal*, Sept. 28, 1962, and William M. Brickman in *Tradition*, Spring, 1961.
22. Herbert Weiner in *Midstream*, Winter, 1962; Milton Himmelfarb in *Commentary*, Jan., 1963.

from the Rights of Man to the Freudian subconscious. Perhaps there was a trace of this desire to end the minority status of the Jew at an earlier turning in history, when a Jew from the diaspora, Saul of Tarsus, envisaged an end of days near at hand in the new dispensation that he had accepted on the road to Damascus, in which there would be "neither Jew nor Greek." The generous promise of modern movements, from liberalism through socialism, was a new world in which there would be neither Jew nor Christian. These ideals were shared not only by Jews who were sacrificing their Judaism on the altars of these new temples to man. Many fervently religious Jews were also partisans of aggressively secularist political movements and of new definitions of culture, because these held out the promise of an end to Jew-hatred.

These hopes were not realized in the home of Western civilization, in Europe. It is not only in the guise of Nazism that the new ideologies have failed the Jews. Communism theoretically abolished anti-Semitism in its new order, but it notoriously persists in Russia, except for a change in terminology. The Jews being persecuted are now guilty of "bourgeois cosmopolitanism" and the synagogue is more harrassed than the Orthodox church because it is a "nest" of this alleged spirit. The liberal anticlerical Third French Republic, after the church was totally disestablished, still did not really produce a situation of equality. Public school classes were never held on Sunday; to this day they are given on Saturday in France; it is therefore at least possible to raise one's children to be Christian without coming into collision with the practices of state institutions, but this is impossible for Jews. Jewish fervor for the modern, secular ideologies has, therefore, by now been tempered by many more or less negative experiences. These movements did not always put an end to anti-Semitism in Europe, where they did achieve power, and in some instances they even gave to hatred of the Jew a greater virulence.

*The encounter of the Jew with America has therefore had unique importance*. This country's attractiveness for the over-

159

whelming majority of Europe's Jews, for both those who succeeded in coming and those who could not, was not merely in its open frontiers and large economic opportunities. America was the home of the one society in the Western world which had no medieval past; here there had never been a ghetto, pogroms, or an anti-Jewish state. The Jew therefore believed that he could share as an equal in the creation of the "new man," the American. If his Exile were truly to come to an end, on every level, somewhere among the gentiles, it could really be "only in America." Here was the last, best hope of the Jew to become a normal part of a national culture. Therefore in the years of the great depression the Jews were the only ethnic group in America which still showed a surplus of immigrants over emigrants.[23] There was deep reason for this, for after un-

23. The statistics on immigration to and emigration from the United States during the years when the impact of the depression was most felt, 1932-1936, are truly startling.

| | Admissions | | Departures | |
|---|---|---|---|---|
| | Total | Jews | Total | Jews |
| 1932 | 35,576 | 2,755 | 103,295 | 452 |
| 1933 | 23,068 | 2,372 | 80,081 | 384 |
| 1934 | 29,470 | 4,134 | 39,771 | 319 |
| 1935 | 34,956 | 4,837 | 38,834 | 330 |
| 1936 | 36,329 | 6,252 | 35,817 | 308 |
| Totals | 159,399 | 20,350 | 297,798 | 1,793 |

In these five years roughly 11 percent of all the immigrants were Jews, but they were less than 1 percent of the emigrants. There was an overall surplus of 138,399 of emigrants over immigrants; Jewish emigration was negligible. This table is adopted from *The American Jewish Year Book* (Philadelphia: Jewish Publication Society, 1943), Vol. 45, p. 592.

The 1930's were, of course, the years of rising Nazi tensions. The actual effect of Hitler's coming to power in 1933 began to be felt in American immigration patterns in the next two years and it rose sharply in 1936 and thereafter. Many tens of thousands more would, of course, have come to the United States had our doors not been virtually barred. What is noteworthy is that for Jews the gathering storms in Europe underscored something which they had known for at least two generations, that they were safer in America and more at home here than anywhere in the Western world. It needs to be added that these figures put a new light on the occasional charge of "dual allegiance" which is sometimes made against the Jews in America. We have now demonstrated that non-Jewish Americans are easier to persuade to abandon this country in a bad economic time, despite the growth of illiberalism elsewhere in the world at that time, than are the Jews. See Salo Baron, in *Publication of the American Jewish Historical Society*, Vol. 44, pp. 199-204.

told wanderings America was, and is, for its Jews not another
way station but an end of the line.

Most Jews are, therefore, committed to something more
than a neutral political state in America, with a Christian culture that gives them a benevolent minority status. In the last
generation they attempted to realize this by helping to imagine
an America of "cultural pluralism." This meant that each
American would live in two cultures, the public culture common to all and the subculture of his own particular ethnic
tradition. This dream was not to be realized, not because the
Jews did not want it but because other ethnic groups chose
to enter the melting pot. The grandchildren of the immigrants
have apparently been keeping only one distinction which
separates them from all other Americans, namely, the religion
(but not the ethnic consciousness) of their ancestors. This fact
was observed and a new wish image, for this day, was projected in Will Herberg's book, *Catholic—Protestant—Jew*.
Though Herberg himself was careful to point out that religion
has, and must have, cultural and societal implications, his suggestions have been assimilated into the public mind as a blue-
print for a secular public culture shared by all Americans, who
will differ only by belonging to three coexisting and equal
enclaves of private religiosity. This vision is exemplified now-
adays at Presidential inaugurations, when clergymen of all
three faiths pray. As is no secret, Jews are much more uplifted
by the presence of rabbis at that occasion than Christians are
by the participation of bishops. For Jews, the matter-of-fact
appearance of a rabbi at the most sacral moment of American
civic life is visual proof that they are indeed equal, in every
sense, and that they do belong as full co-owners of American
culture.

I have given this instance of prayers at the inauguration of
the President by design, to make a further point. It is simply
not true that Jews are completely doctrinaire in their view of
the First Amendment. Chaplains in the armed services, prayers
at state occasions, tax exemptions for religious institutions and
the like are practices which Justice Douglas would now like

to strike down, in the name of intellectual and legal consistency, but he is not here joined by any greater ground swell of Jewish than of Christian opinion. In these areas the Jews really are equal in all respects to all other denominations in America, and no pressure of the majority or of its faith is being exercised upon them. Jews speak absolutely of separation of church and state on those occasions when they are threatened with events or must submit to practices which can be justified only if they were to admit to themselves that their ultimate status in America is that of a most generously tolerated minority. The First Amendment is not the real dogma of the American Jew. His deepest and most messianic need is not a completely secular state; *it is a truly equal status in American culture.*

The battle has been joined in recent years over the place of the Jew in American society with particular militancy and forthrightness because a new generation of Jews has now grown to maturity and is taking over the leadership of that community. This is but one aspect of a process of change which involves the whole of American life, and not merely the Jews. Sociological factors are playing as large a role as historic predispositions or intellectual convictions. Since 1865 some thirty-five million immigrants, the overwhelming majority of them non-Protestant and non-Anglo-Saxon, have poured into this country. The first generation came out of hunger and looked to America for bread. In the next generation, the American-born children of the newcomers, the move from the ghettos began and, with it, some preliminary bids for a political role, at least on the local and state level, and for acceptance in society. Today, the third generation, and even much of the fourth, are full grown. They have no immigrant memories, and they have almost forgotten the languages brought by the grandparents. These men and women are thoroughly assimilated to the dominant moods and modes of contemporary America.

This description fits the situation both of Jews and of Catholics. In the case of both groups the generation represented by

John F. Kennedy will allow no one to tell them that they are less American than the descendants of an older majority. The point was made for the Catholics, in part, by the election of Mr. Kennedy to the Presidency. The wave of their last century of immigration did indeed crest at the White House, but many battles remain before Catholics can remake American society sufficiently to accomodate some of their other needs. Jews cannot hope in any forseeable future to elect a President, but their comparable, native generation is engaged in a similar battle: to remove from public life anything that suggests that they are less at home here than Cabots—or Kennedys.

The real confrontation at this moment is not, therefore, between the Christian defenders of the *status quo* on religion and culture and the Jews, who are supposed to be in more or less uncomfortable league with atheists, secularists, and the like. What is happening today represents attempts from two directions to create change, with the Jewish pressure on the *status quo* really far less important than the Catholic. For one moment in history, on the day that John F. Kennedy was barely elected to the White House, Jewish and Catholic feeling and interests converged. Jews therefore gave a politician for whom, in his own person, they had far less fervor than for Roosevelt the largest majority of their votes that any candidate had ever received. So, of course, did Catholics. Since that day Catholics have not merely intensified their battle for tax aid to parochial schools; they have largely replaced Protestants in the van of the defense of religion in the public schools, the very schools they once abandoned as too godless when much more Christianity was overtly practiced in them than is today. Catholics have indeed largely replaced Protestants as the guardians of the whole complex of practices that was created as a sub-Protestant public piety. Whatever may be the exact intent and purpose of Jewish policy, it is now clearly in conflict with this Catholic drive for a more Christian America. In the sight of this battle, the Protestants have been in process of changing their policy. Before one can suggest a Jewish position for the future, we must therefore discuss in some detail what the present stances of the two major Christian communions appear to mean from a Jewish vantage point.

# III

All the denominations of American Christianity have grown markedly in the postwar years. We therefore tend to imagine that whatever pressure exists for a more Christian America is a reflection of this strength. There are grounds, however, for believing that the reverse is true. In world perspective Christianity has undergone a radical, and negative change in the last two decades, in its relationship with both Communism and with the Eastern faiths. It has suffered enormous losses in central and eastern Europe and in the whole of Asia and Africa. To paraphrase a well known maxim about history, the "domestic policy" of American Christianity must be understood in integral relationship to the difficult situation of the faith in the world as a whole.

The realization of the historic change, in all its shock, has been slow in coming. As recently as 1953, S. C. Carpenter, a prominent English divine, could write that "others are either ignorant of what is happening or strangely blind to the significance of the fact that Asia and Africa are gradually becoming Christian."[24] This was outdated even as it was written. A truer and much more pessimistic estimate was given five years later by an American Protestant analyst, Edmund Perry:

"For the first time in its entire history the Christian faith is on the brink of a decisive encounter with the other major religious systems of the world which are now determined to define the encounter in their own terms. . . . The missionary inroads of Christian faith into these other religions have been made by an offensive church against defensive religions. Henceforth the Church has to meet a counteroffensive by the other religions, for there is a resurgence of vitality especially

24. S. C. Carpenter, *Christianity* (New York: Penguin Books, 1953), p. 151.

164

in Hinduism, Buddhism and Islam, and this resurgence is characterized by a feverish missionary zeal which puts the Church on the defensive. . . . No contemporary devotee of any one of these older faiths is willing to think of his faith as a preliminary faith which should give way to or lead into Christianity. . . . From his point of view, Christians' claims to exclusive truth and grace in the Gospel are the same fabric as the attitude of racial and cultural superiority which characterized the political and economic domination of Asia and Africa by the white man."[25]

Today therefore, for the first time in its history, Christianity is in a "Jewish situation." Judaism has been marked from its beginning by a tension between the universal and the particular, between God who speaks to and about all men and the incarnation of that faith in the particular destiny and needs of the children of Abraham, Isaac, and Jacob, who are its bearers. Christianity appeared in the world announcing itself as the universalism of Judaism, incarnate in the messiah who had come, and stripped of any particular reference to Jew or Greek. But today Christianity is the religion of the West and primarily of whites. It remains, of course, a gospel addressed to all men; and yet it cannot but know that, in the here and now, it is rooted in one geographical area and in one cultural organism.

This situation has enormous bearing on the American scene. As is well known, the Vatican publishes no budget, but it cannot be doubted that its major support today comes from the United States. American involvement is equally important to the Protestant and Orthodox World Council of Churches and to all mission efforts of the individual Protestant denominations. What such facts mean is that in a problematic world, less friendly to Christianity than any recent age, America is now the central support of that faith. It was not always so, for until this very generation what happened in the United States

25. Edmund Perry, *The Gospel in Dispute* (New York: Doubleday, 1958), pp. 16-17.

was of secondary importance to the global outlook of the churches. Today, the battle for influence and growth in America is almost a life-and-death matter for the major Christian communions.

In the face of present dangers there are, in logic, two possible paths for Christian leadership to follow: one is to bend their energies toward strengthening the West, the home of Christianity, and the role of the faith within its culture, in order to give it increased morale for the inevitable battle with the infidels; the other is to attempt to get outside of Western culture by breaking the connection between the faith and its embodiment within any particular society. Each of the great Christian communions is broad enough to contain representatives and tendencies reflecting both outlooks. It is nonetheless fair to say that, in America, Catholic policy is overwhelmingly committed to the first alternative. The Protestant outlook is more diffuse, but it is increasingly showing signs of movement away from identifying Christianity more closely with the West in general and America in particular.[26]

There is not, of course, one Protestantism in this country but rather several major and often antithetical strands. The conservative, fundamentalist variety is well-nigh a state church in the South. The devotion of most such Protestants to the First Amendment is in evidence, as it was during the 1960 election, as a form of anti-Catholic nativism. These Protestants are against any aid to parochial schools, on the grounds of separation of church and state, but they are equally violent against any attempt to remove Christian practices from the schools. So in an early stage of one of the several such cases now being litigated, in the suit in Miami, Florida, against Christmas celebrations in the schools and the like, the local Protestant Council of Churches spoke through its president: "I can see no reason why we should turn to a pagan concept

26. The most recent exposition of the changing Protestant view is in Franklin Littell, *From Church State to Pluralism* (New York: Doubleday, 1962).

of life when we profess to be a Christian nation."[27] By and large, such thinking is most prevalent in those segments of American Protestantism which, even though they do support missionaries, are almost oblivious to the world outside of America.

At the other extreme of theological sophistication and international awareness, there stand some intellectual leaders of the historic Protestant churches who are for the absolute separation of church and state not because they are grudgingly yielding to outside pressures but for very positive religious reasons. Men like Franklin Littell are eager for a Protestantism that is entirely free of any hampering relationship to American culture and American patriotism, so that the church may become unambiguously what it ought to be, the critic and the conscience of society. In such opinions there are overtones of Roger Williams and of the thought of the leading contemporary expounder of an ever-reforming, individualistic, critical "Protestant principle," Paul Tillich. The influence of the European theologian, Karl Barth, is also beginning to be felt. His version of Protestantism is a waiting for the "end of days," in considerable indifference to whichever society may make the Christian unhappy at the moment. Such thinking is present in the underpinnings of the position recently suggested to the United Presbyterian Church: "Theologically, the church must be aware that the sole constant in its mandate is the fact of Jesus Christ. It is to the Christ that the church bears witness, not to a theological articulation of the place of the political order in the structure of reality."[28] Therefore, in the section of practical recommendations, the authors of this document can go so far as to suggest that, in the matter of tax exemption for religious agencies, "the church must regard special status or favored position as a hindrance to the fulfilling of its mission."[29]

27. See my article in *Commentary* for Oct., 1960.
28. *Relations Between Church and State*, p. 38.
29. *Ibid.*, p. 19.

This report is, at the moment of writing, a study document and not an officially adopted position. Whatever the destiny of this particular set of suggestions may be, I do not believe that they represent the main thrust of American Protestantism. The "stated clerk" of this very denomination, Eugene Carson Blake, spoke quite differently during the campaign of 1960, when he was fearful of a Roman Catholic in the White House, because "a Protestant President is free to participate in the many interfaith activities that have been built up so carefully over the years. But a Roman Catholic is not."[30] Obviously, even in the heat of that turbulent summer, when some things were said which would perhaps now be put differently, Dr. Blake knew that going to interfaith occasions is not a constitutional duty of the President. What he had in mind is an image of our culture in which the various sects are treated as equals, and religion as a whole is in some deep sense the American establishment. It is in that spirit that Bishop James Pike deplored the decision in the Regents' prayer case. Perhaps the most significant reactions to the action of the Supreme Court come from Reinhold Niebuhr and John C. Bennett. These two leaders of liberal opinion among Protestants on interreligious and social issues surprised some people by not supporting the Court's strictly separationist stand. Niebuhr held that "the prayer seemed to be a model of accomodation to the pluralistic nature of our society" and he deplored that the result would be a "consistently secular education that the Founding Fathers certainly did not intend."[31] Bennett, in agreement with these views, urged "the Court to define the church-state problem in less absolutistic terms than those to which it is inclined."[32]

Perhaps the best summary of this entire outlook was given by William Lee Miller a few years ago. "The main stream of religion here has not emphasized repudiation of the principalities and powers of this world or withdrawal from society in

30. *Commentary*, Oct., 1960.
31. *Christianity and Crisis*, July 23, 1962.
32. *Ibid.*, Aug. 6, 1962.

order to preserve ethical purity and holiness. . . . It has tried to embrace the whole society and not be compromised with its evil; it has tried to deal seriously with the problems of power even while it attained great power. . . . This tradition countenances no desire for a 'religious' state or even an officially religious society; it does, however, want a religious people and an unofficially religious society." Miller saw the mainstream of religion in America broadening through various forms of Protestantism "into a tolerant common religiosity with three faith compartments."[33] What this stance amounts to is the affirming of two propositions: that religion is indeed quasi-established in America and that the terms of that establishment include only such practices and restrictions which put the historic faiths on a plane of equality. Though the Protestants quoted above would differ in detail, this attitude would probably construct a public policy on religion in American life along the following lines: there should be teaching about religion in the schools, as a fact of culture; experimenting with "shared time"; the Bible should at least be read in the schools, but sectarian practices like Christmas celebrations and the Lord's Prayer should be excluded; and though some blue laws should perhaps be kept, there should be legal exemptions for Sabbath observers. Out of this stance the continued presence on the books of Massachusetts and Connecticut of laws against contraception is deplored, but there is growing concern, in the name of fairness, for the great burden borne by Catholics in support of their ever larger and ever more expensive network of parochial schools.

Jews might wish to argue with one or the other of the "planks" in such a platform. All of the official Jewish bodies have often pointed out that "common core" curricula, or other forms of teaching religion in the schools, tend to be Christian-oriented, simply because of the fact that most of the teachers are themselves products of that tradition. Many Jews prefer an

33. William Lee Miller in *Religion and the Free Society* (New York: The Fund for the Republic, 1958), p. 18.

end to blue laws, because the process of securing exemptions for Sabbath observers inevitably involves questioning by state agencies of the religious sincerity of the individual requesting such an exception for himself. Nonetheless, this position in essence meets a basic need of the main body of American Jews. It grants their cherished desire for a tri-faith image of America, and, underlying it, is a concept of a religious consensus based, at least consciously, not on lowest-common-denominator Christianity but on the biblical values common to both Judaism and Christianity. Reinhold Niebuhr's views, as one of the architects of this stance, are really consonant with a theological suggestion that he made a few years ago, that Christianity cease all missionary activity among the Jews and accept the notion that each of the two biblical faiths is an equally valid divine revelation for its believers. A new theology thus was created to provide the basis of a consensus in practice.

Niebuhr's critics, who were in the majority among the theologians, did not accept the change in theology that he suggested. They were, and are, loath to part with the idea that in an ultimate sense Christianity is the true faith for all men. They pointed out, negatively, that such views would inevitably have to stretch further to end the missions to all the other major faiths, thus leaving Christianity permanently as one among many religions. Whatever may be the theological virtues, or lack of them, of Niebuhr's views, they are the only possible non-Barthian approach to living with a plurality of sects in the world. It is a pragmatic, American kind of answer to the "foreign policy" question posed for Christianity in the postwar world.

The majority, which does not accept this theory, must make a greater effort to come to terms with a tri-faith consensus in practice, for it entails the strain of seriously denying oneself the right to do within society that which he feels he must do. It can, and has been argued, for example, on theological grounds that to help create a situation in the schools where Jewish children hear nothing of Jesus is a failure in love, for it means that the Christian is not sharing his greatest treasure with others. Nonetheless, the sharpness of the Jewish-Protestant encounter on church-state matters is lessening. The self-denying bargain that, as I maintained above, was the essential promise demanded from the denominations by American society as the price of their freedom is being ever more understood among Protestants in relation to Jewish sensitivities.

The encounter with Catholics is an entirely different matter. Protestantism has been living for centuries, since its beginning, with division, and it has been accustomed from its earliest days to a theology in which none of its individual churches is absolute. To stretch that doctrine further so that no faith is regarded as absolute, or even to live with other faiths in practice on the level of complete equality, is a long next step—but it is one step, and not two. The Catholic faith maintains the much more circumscribed doctrine of the one "true church." In the present ecumenical movement the Roman church is making the beginning of a major adjustment, to thinking of other Christian groups as not completely invalid; it is moving some distance, even in theology, toward the Protestant position on the equality of the churches. No theological approach at all, beyond the doctrine of the rights prudently to be given error, has however yet been suggested to validate the equality, in theory, of all faiths. The Catholic church is not at all individualistic, and it has always believed that, where prudential reasons do not dictate a contrary policy, it should dominate culture. It is, therefore, really being asked to go against what seems, to the outsider, to be its very nature, if it were to accept all the implications of a self-limiting pledge.

Even here something is stirring. John Courtney Murray is far too much of a Catholic classicist even to imagine that, theologically, there is any religion other than his own that is ultimately true, but he has moved appreciatively toward the other faiths: "There may indeed be some three hundred religious bodies in America. But there are not that many 'styles' of religious belief. In fact, there are generically only three—

171

the Protestant, the Catholic, and the Jewish. They are radically different 'styles' and no one of them is reducible, or perhaps even comparable, to any of the others. And in each case the style of the epistemology of faith is related to the structure of the theology (or possibly to the absence of a theology)."[34]

To the outside observer, however, Catholic policy in America seems to be determined more by other considerations. The recent anger in some Catholic circles, reaching to the very top of the hierarchy in America, over the decision in *Engel* v. *Vitale* could not really have been occasioned by the excision of a short prayer of little, if any, religious significance. No doubt the great problem of the future financing of the parochial schools came immediately to Catholic minds, for Federal money seemed more remote after that decision was handed down. Both these themes were clearly linked in Cardinal Spellman's statement on the case, although his most important concern was for maintaining and indeed increasing the Christian flavor of American culture. The Founding Fathers, in the Cardinal's view, did not intend "to establish irreligion"; such actions as the prohibition of the Regents' prayer tend to "the establishment of a new religion of secularism."[35] The same attitude was reflected a few months before in Boston, when the *Pilot*, the official paper of the diocese of Cardinal Cushing, was even more vehement about a suggested breach in the blue laws. The Senate of Massachusetts had already passed a bill excepting all Sabbath observers, whatever their business, from the prohibition to keep open on Sunday. The editorial in the *Pilot* was willing to concede this right to establishments purveying kosher food, and the like, primarily to Jews, but it called any further liberalization a "shocking assault," "unjust and offensive," and evidence that a "carefully organized minority has done its work to destroy the Sunday." It went beyond even this charged language to print a list of

34. Murray, *ibid.*, p. 138.
35. *New York Times*, Aug. 3, 1962.

the senators who had voted for the bill, clearly asking that pressure be brought upon them.[36] (It was, and the bill was rescinded.) In the heat of that moment it was forgotten in Boston that in 1960, in the crucial last week of the presidential election campaign, Cardinal Cushing had assured the country that the hierarchy would never dictate to voters on any issue.[37]

More contradictions of like nature can be pointed out. It is admitted on all sides that the bill for major Federal aid to education has been defeated, so far, by pressure brought to bear on the members of Congress by the Catholic hierarchy.[38] In another important action during the campaign of 1960, a leading Jesuit theologian, Father Gustave Weigel and a group of Catholic scholars gave the following assurances: American Catholics "do not want the religious freedom of American non-Catholics to be curtailed in any way. They sincerely want the present First Amendment to be retained and become

36. *Boston Pilot*, June 9, 1962.
37. *New York Times*, Oct. 28, 1960.
38. On Nov. 16, 1961, the National Catholic Welfare Conference issued a statement on behalf of the American Bishops in which they "reaffirmed their stand against any form of general federal aid to education that discriminates against children attending non-public schools." The Bishops asked for "objective study of the need and of the possible effects of such aid on American social structure and institutions." What is noteworthy in that statement is that no attempt was made to claim such aid as a legal right under the First Amendment. The appeal was in the name of what Father Murray calls "distributive justice." This of course raises the very real issue as to whether, if we are to discuss the matter in terms of what is good for society, it is indeed good for society for our public school system to disappear and be replaced by a network of privately organized schools. Will such a change then, apart from its obvious social divisiveness, not also bring in its train the possibility of a new method of racially segregating the schools?

That this statement did indeed apply political pressure very directly to Congress was not doubted even by Catholics. See, for example, the article by Justus George Lawler, in *Commonweal* for Jan. 26, 1962: "The hierarchy, of course, should have spoken out; but they should have spoken as informed advisors rather than as churchmen enunciating decrees. That in some cases they chose the latter course, that in some cases they implied the possibility of using their ecclesiastical power to launch reprisals against the proponents of federal aid to public education exclusively, was at the least—given the state of public opinion—imprudent, and at the most an exorbitant extension of their office."

ever more effective."[39] This attitude is clearly not the present view of Cardinal Spellman. He was recently represented before the Senate Judiciary Committee by a plea in favor of a constitutional amendment which would not only permit nondenominational prayers in the schools but would specifically include other "traditional practices," like Christmas celebrations.[40]

It is easy to prolong this exercise in cross-examination by quotation and thereby to arrive at two judgments: that the "liberal" views were campaign oratory and that there is a continuing Catholic drive to "dominate" (whatever that word may mean in this context) America. Both estimates are false. The Catholic "liberals" are still in evidence, and their numbers are probably growing; the conspiratorial theory is too obviously nonsense to require refutation. What, then, are the underlying issues?

It seems to me that the policy of the official leaders of the Catholic church in America is to be explained in the light of their wider conceptions of the future of American society and of America's role in the world. Within America they are seriously (and from their point of view, it must be said, rightly) fearful of "indifferentism," the sin of believing that one religion is as good as another. Today this may be a view that only Reinhold Niebuhr and Paul Tillich, among the theologians, approach, but it does in a very untheoretical way pervade American consciousness. It is imparted in many ways in the public schools. Jews may find that this "religion" of belief in religion is too Christian, but precisely because of its Christian origins, it is not unrelated to the Catholic faith; it is, therefore, doubly dangerous to Catholics. The line from the middle of the nineteenth century, when Catholics fought for the First Amendment, to today is really straight; it is the policy of keeping Catholics out of an "indifferentist" consensus. The major difference is that today the Roman Church is both

39. *New York Times*, Sept. 28, 1960.
40. *New York Times*, Oct. 12, 1962.

strong enough, in numbers and in generations of rootedness in America, and weak enough, in the overextension of its economic resources, to make a fight of it for a different kind of America, in which it hopes to win tax support for creating "a truly pluralist educational order."[41]

The even larger concern which permeates the Catholic position is Communism. If Christianity as a whole has lost heavily in recent decades, the Catholic church has lost more than the Protestant. Many of the countries which are now satellites, like Poland and Hungary, were mostly bastions of Catholic strength. Therefore, the danger from Communism is most immediate to the heaviest losers. To the Catholic mind, schooled as it is to think in terms of faith and dogma, its confrontation with Communism is a war of ideas, between religion and antireligion. It therefore seems self-evident to Catholics to imagine that this is equally true of the political confrontation between the Communist and non-Communist worlds. America, as the leader of the West, is cast for the role of the knightly defender of the faith. For America to be true to this sacred mission the Christian nature of public life must therefore be shored up. Parochial schools will teach the Catholics; the rest must get at least enough indoctrination in the public schools so that they will appreciate the trust for which they must battle. One cannot yield on this matter, for there is at stake the morale and sense of purpose of the West in the great battle of this century.

It is here that I must dissent most strongly. This notion is not merely utterly wrong in its conception of the meaning of the Cold War. Should it ever win assent in America, it would sow the seed of our certain defeat and disaster. Our age should not be made into a new seventeenth century, a time of "wars of religion." The peoples of Asia and Africa will respond to our American leadership only if what we offer as a counterfaith to Communism is not Christianity or even Judeo-Christianity, but rather the greatest of all American values: the

41. Lawler, *ibid*.

vision of a world order in which all men serve side by side and help each other to be true to themselves, to their own hopes and aspirations.

Let me add that in the next century American society and indeed the whole Western world will inevitably tend to become pluralist in a much more complex way than ever before. A few years ago America took the first step toward opening the door of immigration to Asiatics and Africans by assigning modest quotas to that part of the world. And now it has admitted Hawaii to statehood. That means that more and more Buddhists, Hindus, and Moslems will come to our shores, because America cannot be true either to itself or to its responsibilities if it refuses them entry. The pluralism of our society will therefore have to take on a different cast. No longer will it be merely Jewish-Christian or religious-secular. Our society will have to devise a framework in which religions essentially foreign to each other will be able to meet in the common marketplace of an America which is steadily becoming a microcosm of all humanity.

Roman Catholics are, however, not alone in proposing an ideological definition of the Cold War, and of wanting to bend American culture into the shape of such a definition. The Communists themselves see the present as a struggle between their idea and capitalism. The secularists, the frequent whipping boys of the Roman Catholic press, also generally see the situation in the same way. For them it is a war between democracy, which they tend to define as a body of positive and commanding doctrine, and its ideological antithesis. What was the nineteenth century secularist idea of the *mission civilisatrice* of Europe in Africa and Asia, if not liberalism as conversionist faith, if need be with fire and sword?

All of these faiths, both religious and secular, exemplify a basic cast of the Western mind. The precision of Aristotelian logic and the beauty of the Platonic ideas have implanted within it an enchantment with tidiness and with abstractions. Life is, however, concrete and diffuse; it is very untidy and its stuff does not fit easily into definitions. There is always something *ad hoc* about its solutions. Doctrines are signposts for society, not its blueprints. We must, therefore, eschew holy wars; we must accept and live with untidiness and ambiguity. This is the key to peace in our own age both within American society and the world as a whole.

It is no accident that at the beginnings of Jewish modernity, after the American and French revolutions, advanced spirits among the Jews were so taken with ideologies. The reason was not only that the ideologies promised a new society transcending the hatreds which had created the centuries of exclusion of the Jews. It was also that instinctively the Jews felt that attachment to ideology was a characteristic Western mode of thinking and acting. Their acceptance of secular, Western, dogmatic "religions" was the first, profound form of their acculturation. At its deepest, this is what the abandonment of the Talmudic academy for the European university meant. The Jew is really, however, the product of a tradition which is intellectually not ideological. Only for Aristotle is A not non-A. The classic Jew can be at one and the same time a bearer of a universal religion and a particular national tradition, a member of the "chosen people" and the possessor of no special rights or qualities. His history, too, is equally unlogical. Tidy countries and ages have always attempted to do away with the Jew, in the name of order. He has flourished where the intellectual rationales of rulers have been tempered by pragmatic common sense.

In the America of today the Jew cannot, of course, join the Catholic concepts of America and the West. He must be equally warned against "First Amendmentism." Any dogma taken to the extreme is ultimately the enemy of freedom and, as he should by now have relearned from his experience with modern ideologies, it is the enemy of the Jew. It is possible to rule more things than blue laws into the secular, civic content of American life, and then turn such rules against one or another faith. Constitutional logic alone might not keep some future generation from opening the public schools on Saturday for the purpose of intensifying education. Only the untidiness of intergroup arrangement, compromise, and, sometimes, counterpressure could prevent it.

Most immediately, within American society itself, some Jews, along with some Protestants, are committed to the parochial school and are therefore in agreement with Catholics on this issue. This alliance should no more be mistaken as permanent and dogmatic than the counteralliance of most of organized Jewry with secularists in support of a strict interpretation of the First Amendment. The most eminent of Jewish dignitaries to deplore the Supreme Court's decision in *Engel* v. *Vitale* in the name of the need for prayer, Rabbi Menachem Schneerson, has nonetheless addressed himself with outrage to the Catholic activists for their "thinly veiled warnings in the direction of the Jewish community." He went further, to suggest to the Catholic hierarchy that when there is disagreement between these two communities it must disavow anything said in its quarters that appears to Jews as threatening them with anti-Semitism.[42]

Religious statesmanship knows no more permanent alliances than those that prevail in secular life. What is permanent are the continuing intents and needs of each of the faiths. So, the most parochial and orthodox of Jews may agree with others that there is need for more religion in public life, but he will recoil when this need is fulfilled in such fashion as to add an iota to the coercive power of the Christian majority over him.

Statesmanship even of the highest order cannot really determine events, even within the confines of each denomination. American society is too diffuse, and our churches and synagogues reflect that diffuseness too much, for any real control to be exercised over the order in which battles arise. I venture that most of Jewish leadership would have preferred that the use of the Regents' Prayer had not been litigated

42. See Rabbi Menachem M. Schneerson's letter to *The Jewish Forum*, Hanukah, 1962.

before the Supreme Court when it was. If the time was ripe then for the removal of some sectarian practices from the schools, specifically Christian ones, like Christmas observances, would have been of greater concern than a nondenominational prayer. In the continuing argument which revolves around the Bible and the recitation of the Lord's Prayer in the classrooms, Jews can accept, and perhaps many even want, the former. My own feeling is that the Bible occupies so central a place in our civilization that not to have its content and cadences bred into one's bones is to be undereducated. However the shelter of the First Amendment is meant not only for minorities in the Biblical tradition. The task of teaching the Bible had, therefore, best be left to religious institutions of the various persuasions. Even the present pervasive procedure of reading some verses, without comment, in the morning in school clearly does exercise pressure on the children of agnostics, and it does not begin to teach the Bible adequately to the children of believers. In the second place, we can still maintain today that the Bible is crucial to the whole of American experience. This is less likely to be true in the next century, when non-Biblical peoples will be more largely represented here. Jews are therefore opposed, but no more so than many others, to Bible reading in the schools. The Lord's Prayer, is, however, another matter; it is specifically Christian and its recitation in the schools is clearly, even in today's America, a sectarian practice, which all Jews, without exception, are committed to opposing.

So many of the present controversies around church and state revolve around the schools for the obvious reason that, more than any other institution, it is the school that shapes our culture. There is, to be sure, a minority within the Jewish community which is totally committed to, or somewhat colored by, a desire to stand apart from American society and which therefore is not really involved in the public school. For the majority the public school is no matter-of-course institution; it is the major place where they visibly experience their integration into America. Jews are therefore perhaps the strongest defenders of public education. The arguments about whether the public school is secular or secularist (it is in truth neither) is irrelevant. The influence of the American intellectual and civic tradition is largely exercised as much by the atmosphere as by the teaching of public education. Everyone is today committed to pluralism, but do we want a completely fragmented America? The unity which binds our diversities into a viable society is largely the creation of the one place where most Americans do spend a crucial part of their lives together. If parochial education, and private, class-ridden schools were to become the norm for America, we would be erecting a society of coexisting ghettos. This is not to say that some parochial education will not, and should not, continue to exist, but most Jews do not wish it to become their dominant educational form, or the dominant form for all Americans.

Discussions of religion and culture tend to dwell so largely on the questions which divide the faiths that we may tend to forget how much unites them. This unity is not in theological dogma, but in social policy. No major religious group in America is racist; all are devoted to a democratic order in politics; and the social justice pronouncements of the major faiths are indistinguishable from each other. These agreements demonstrate that it is far easier to achieve consensus in action than in thought or even in prayer. This observation is congruent with the entire nature of the American tradition, with its tentativeness and its emphasis on the needs of the day. As a Jew I am certainly most at home in this atmosphere, because the whole of my tradition points toward the equality of all faiths, even in theory, and to their being able to join together in practice for moral ends.

Perhaps the only description that fits the complicated pattern in which law, the American tradition, and the faiths are interwoven is in the not very grandiloquent but saving phrase "not quite." Religion is neither established nor completely disestablished in America. There is separation of church and state but it is not absolute. Nothing is more obvious than that there is a body of attitudes which are the American tradition, shaping and to some extent remaking the faiths, but this tradition is neither doctrinaire nor is there common assent as to its exact content. Jews interacting with this situation are also characterized by a "not quite." Certainly in America they are no longer in Exile, in any of the older meanings of the word; nonetheless they are not quite cofounders of American culture. In most relationships they are "just like everybody else"; for some they are uniquely different.

I suspect that if I knew the interior history of other groups in America, even of the oldest and most native of its denominations, some version of "not quite" would be true, for no identity is exactly like another. The Founding Fathers once gave us a clue in the First Amendment as to how to live with such complications in an undogmatic way. Let us not do to one another that which is hateful to any of us. Let us stand separately for our various truths. Let us stand together for the peace of society.